The Education System in Mexico

The Education System in Mexico

David Scott, C. M. Posner,
Chris Martin and Elsa Guzman

UCLPRESS

First published in 2018 by
UCL Press
University College London
Gower Street
London WC1E 6BT

Available to download free: www.ucl.ac.uk/ucl-press

A CIP catalogue record for this book is available from The British Library.

ISBN: 978–1–78735–077–9 (Hbk.)
ISBN: 978–1–78735–076–2 (Pbk.)
ISBN: 978–1–78735–072–4 (PDF)
ISBN: 978–1–78735–073–1 (epub)
ISBN: 978–1–78735–074–8 (mobi)
ISBN: 978–1–78735–075–5 (html)
DOI: https://doi.org/10.14324/111.9781787350724

Preface

In 2013, the Mexican Secretary for Public Education, Emilio Chuayffet, visited the Institute of Education, University of London, to discuss his reforms to the education system in Mexico. He was at this time responsible for all matters concerning education in his country, supported by the Mexican Secretariat of Public Education (Secretaría de Educación Pública, SEP). In particular, he wanted to talk about the recent introduction of a national standard for reading ability that was subsequently rolled out across the system. This was that all children within the state system were to be assessed on the number of words they could read aloud in the classroom in one minute. The number of words was to be increased from one grade to the next. This was devised as a measure to raise standards in the system. In response, we quietly suggested that reading skills could not be measured in this way, that this would lead to a distortion of the reading process and that almost certainly more children would develop a lifelong aversion to reading. Unfortunately, our protestations had little effect and the scheme was introduced in Mexican schools with the results that we had anticipated and warned about. This is an example of a standards and accountability approach that now holds sway in most parts of the world, and in particular in Mexico and is enthusiastically endorsed by international bodies, such as the World Bank and the Organisation for Economic Co-operation and Development (OECD).

This book is a result of a long immersion in the country by three of the four authors. More formally, it has emerged from our work, funded by the Mexican Government, to identify a set of standards in Literacy, Numeracy and Science/Technology, to develop systems and procedures for ensuring the implementation and sustainability of these standards mechanisms, and to contribute to more effective schooling and a better trained and educated workforce in Mexico. The project attempted to provide answers to the following questions: What are appropriate standards in Literacy, Numeracy and Science/Technology at different age and ability levels for Mexico? What are appropriate contents, progressions, skills/dispositions and formative and summative assessment arrangements in the domains of Literacy, Numeracy and Science/Technology, for the Mexican education system? Which external and internal school arrangements are best suited for their implementation? What is the most appropriate way to sustain these reforms (new curriculum standards in Literacy, Numeracy and Science/Technology and the arrangements for their implementation and use)? (See also Scott et al., 2012)

During this process, we encountered all the familiar difficulties of conducting any research project in any part of the world, and in addition, we encountered two particularly Mexican issues. The first we can briefly describe here as the repeated failures of the Mexican government to implement meaningful and sustainable system-wide reforms of educational institutions. (We examine this issue in much greater detail in the book.) The second issue is the way all discussions in Mexico about education are politicized and, as a result and more so than in many other countries round the world, emptied of significance. This is the background to our writing this book, which we hope makes a contribution to a better understanding of educational institutions in Mexico and consequently better practices within the system.

David Scott
C. M. Posner
Chris Martin
Elsa Guzman
25 June 2017

Contents

1 Introduction and a Brief History of the Mexican Education System

It is customary to speak of a group of schools as a *system* and indeed there is a great deal of sense in this for the reasons we explain further on. However, describing education as a system risks ignoring the core of that activity, namely, that it is a series of profoundly personal acts of learning. Thus, from the outset, any consideration of the Mexican education system also needs to take into account the tension between the drive to learn and the systematic attempt to organize and control it. The root of this tension lies in the difference between the basic demand for access to learning opportunities for the satisfaction of needs (emotional, spiritual, material and intellectual) and the control and selection processes that education systems undertake.

Comparative educationalists have traditionally studied national education systems, with a notion of comparison between systems or within individual systems being the dominant methodological device. The field was first developed in the early nineteenth century in parallel with the rise of national education systems, and it took the national system as its main object of enquiry (Noah and Eckstein, 1969). Some have argued that this approach is now redundant, since nation states are declining and national systems are consequently becoming obsolete (Reich, 2015). Indeed, the very idea of a system is anachronistic in a world of global markets, multinational, transnational or even stateless corporations and cross-national comparative systems of evaluation and control. The thrust of our argument in this book is that nation states and national systems of education are far from redundant and even in single nation studies comparison still has a role to play.

Education systems change over time and they experience alterations to both their internal and external structures and relations.

Whether change occurs or not depends on the capacity within the system as well as the condition of the change-catalyst or set of reforms. These are structured in particular ways, and this determines their ability to act as change-agents. Certain types of catalyst are more likely to induce change in a system than others; for example, changes of personnel (caused naturally through retirements and deaths or by people in powerful positions within the system exercising their authority), new policies, events in nature, external interventions, new arrays of resources, new arrangements of roles and functions within a system, new financial settlements and so forth. In short, some of these change-catalysts are – or at least have the potential to be – more powerful than others. Even here though, the catalyst's capacity to effect change within a system cannot guarantee or determine whether change actually occurs. We can see this most clearly in some of the reform processes undertaken in Mexico, such as the enactment of the General Law of Service in the Teaching Profession (Ley General del Servicio Profesional Docente (LGSPD)), which was passed in September 2013 (Government of Mexico, 2013). This provided the legal framework for reforming the system of education, including the provision of new mechanisms for professional development, recruitment, promotion and the recognition of qualifications. It replaced the Carrera Magisterial and was published in May 2015 (Coordinación Nacional del Servicio Profesional Docente (CNSPD)). As we will see, even a reform or change process as comprehensive as this cannot guarantee or determine the degree and type of change within the system, how long lasting the reform is and any unexpected consequences there may be. Furthermore, some types of change-catalyst are more likely to be successful in inducing change within the system than others. This is not only because some interventions in education systems are more powerful than others but also because their capacity to induce change fits better the change mechanism within the system being reformed.

For example, in a system that has a high level of command structure between the coordinating body and its constituent parts, a policy for change at the classroom level underpinned by a strong system of rewards and sanctions is likely to be successful in inducing change at this level. This is in contrast to systems which grant greater degrees of autonomy to their teachers, and consequently the same change mechanism may have less chance of succeeding. Extra-national change agents work in the same way and the Organisation for Economic Co-operation and Development's (OECD's) system of international assessment (known as the Programme for International Student Assessment (PISA)) is an example of this. Mexico has underperformed in PISA every time since it decided to take part. These globalizing bodies, such as the OECD, are attempting to establish a form of global panopticism where the activities of the various national systems are made visible to a supranational body, with the consequence that all parts of the system are visible from one single point. However, what this needs is a single surface of comparison or at least a comparative mechanism, so that enough people have confidence in it for it to be considered useful.

What we have been doing here is categorizing an education system as a set of institutions and relations between its parts, and even perhaps as a coordinating body for a number of subsystems, which have a particular relation to the central authority and a particular position within it. However, this doesn't mean that the central authority and the schools (and its internal and external relations between these and other extra-systemic authorities) remain the same over time. These relations may change for a number of reasons, for example, the invention of new ideas, natural progression, contradictions as historically accumulating structural tensions between open activity systems (see also Engeström, 2001) and so forth. It is possible to characterize education systems along a series of continua: restrictive control by the central authority over its constituent parts as opposed to loose control over these parts or centralized as opposed to decentralized systemic relations; strongly defined notions of expertise as against weakly defined notions; specializations of functions and roles within the system rather than general capacities and clearly defined external relations with other bodies and systems as against weakly defined externalities. There is another important factor to consider: those relations between formal and informal elements of the system that in some instances are pivotal. The relationship between the formal and informal is complex in countries such as Mexico and can only be brought to light through the detailed and deeply immersed case-study approach we adopt in this book.

It is fairly easy then to understand an education system as a coordinating body that directs a number of subunits, so that if the central authority demands action of a particular type, then these subsidiary bodies will implement its directives. The cohering element in the notion of a system being used here is that one body commands a series of other bodies, though all of them are considered to be elements of a system. However, it is rare for any actual system to function in this way. Within the system the extent and type of power that the coordinating body can exercise over the other elements may be exercised in a different way. Thus, a system's coordinating body may have more or less direct relations with different parts of the system. Indeed, it may be that some of these relations become so attenuated that it becomes harder to include them in the system. Private language schools in Mexico are an example.

Furthermore, systems have internal rules, that is, their elements are arranged in particular ways. Traditional systems have a high degree of specialization; a clearly defined division of labour; the distribution of official tasks within the organization; a hierarchical structure of authority with clearly defined areas of responsibility; formal rules which regulate the operation of the organization; a written administration; a clear separation between what is official and what is personal and recruitment on the basis of ability and technical knowledge. However, regardless of how we understand the notion of a system, any change to it is always a transformation of the status quo, to a greater or lesser degree.

In this book, we are interested in all aspects of policy implementation and system change: pedagogical, organizational, epistemic, socio-political and institutional. Critical accounts of policy developments and policy implementations in Mexico will be used to demonstrate that we take particularly seriously the hitherto neglected category of institutional and political infrastructure. But at every point our examination of the non-educational (political) aspects of the bureaucracy will point to the desired educational outcomes and the failure or success of bringing these about.

It is important to start with a framework for educational implementation, a checklist of necessary elements and steps that condition and contextualize the processes of implementation. More recent education policy researchers, such as Stephen Ball (1994), depict curriculum reform and policymaking as a messy, complex and contested enterprise. As has been frequently observed (for example, Whitty et al., 1998), policy is an object of contest and struggle between competing ideologies, education visions, personal interests and political or organizational positions. All of these forces come together in an incubator of international, national and local contexts. For Ball, understanding education reforms requires us to interrogate policy cycles, policy discourses, policy actors, policy arenas and contexts. His is a nuanced and more realistic approach to analysing education reform developed over years through a series of empirical analyses of policy sites, discourses and contexts. Policy is produced through a series of struggles involving many actors and agencies. In addition, local policy cannot be understood without reference to the global impact of transnational agencies such as the Organisation for Economic Co-operation and Development (OECD), the United Nations Educational Scientific and Cultural Organization (UNESCO), the United

Nations Children's Fund (UNICEF), the World Bank, non-profit and for-profit organizations, and so forth.

In trying to understand how interventions in education systems work, in the first instance we need to remind ourselves of the principal elements of a public educational practice, namely, that it comprises the state's deployment of human resources, its strategic hold over infrastructure and other material and financial resources, its mobilization of ceremonies, rituals, meanings and values and its creation and maintenance of a central value system. Therefore, in trying to understand how national education systems, such as the Mexican system and its curriculum, change, we need to understand how the Mexican system and its curriculum was then structured. Thus, the same programme of reform delivered in different countries is likely to have different effects on the different elements of the system and will have different histories within the system. What we have been identifying here are internal relations in a change process.

There are also exogenous or extra-national influences, although we have to be clear that these globalizing pressures do not determine policy and practice within these countries. Globalization comprises a process of policy and practice convergence between different nations, regions and jurisdictions in the world. This can occur in a number of ways. The first is through a process of policy borrowing or policy learning, where the individual country, Mexico for example, is the recipient of policies from other countries or from a collection of other countries. These processes impact in complex ways on educational practices, and not only on state-sponsored ones. The second is through the direct impact of supranational bodies which have power and influence over member countries and which are seeking harmonization of national educational policies and practices. The third is a subtler approach and this is where the supranational body does not deal in policies or practices but in a common currency of comparison, which may be epistemic (as in the means used by, for example, the OECD to compare one education system with another) or functional (as in the distribution of resources, including discursive resources). The fourth process that potentially allows convergence is the autochthonous response of each national system of education to a common imperative from outside its jurisdiction. In most cases this is more likely to encourage divergence rather than convergence. The fifth is a direct response to globalization pressures by a nation, region or jurisdiction, such as the recent decision by the European Commission to fine Google 2.42 billion euros ($2.7bn; £2.1bn) after it ruled that the company had abused its power by promoting its own shopping comparison service at the top of its search results. With regards to the influence and impact of globalization, there are four possible spatio-temporal positioners: the extension and extensive capacity of the global network, its intensity, the velocity of the global flows and the impact they are likely to have (see also Held et al., 1999). In our analysis of these globalizing pressures, we borrow a notion of vernacular globalization from Lingard (2000), which pays careful attention to national, regional and jurisdictional autochthonous responses to the various forms of globalization that currently exist.

In this book we trace the history, effects and significance of the Mexican educational system, reminding ourselves all the time that our understanding of this system has to be contextualized within our chosen methodological approach. This approach emphasizes empirically grounded, detailed and deeply immersed, case-based research; pays careful attention to processes and the temporal dimensions of these in contexts that in some respects are unique to the Mexican setting and offers up comparisons both within and outside the system. In so far as we are adopting a specific methodological position, we can formulate this in the following way. In the first instance, having construed causal laws as expressions of the tendencies of natural and social objects, we resolved all the concrete events and empirical happenings in relation to the workings of the Mexican education system into their components or elements. We re-described or reconfigured each of these components or elements in theoretically significant ways, so as to avoid the de-theorization implicit in some reductive and quantitative-based studies. (For an example of these studies, see also Green and Janmaat, 2014.) The next stage we embarked on was to move from describing the components of these significant events and happenings to proposing explanations about what produces or are the conditions for them. This is the retroductive process (see also Bhaskar, 2010). From this we sought to eliminate alternative possible explanations and identify coherent ones. Finally, we corrected or at least offered corrections to earlier proposed explanations in light of our analysis, thus in the process delineating the parameters of our explanations and how these relate to the ontology and epistemology of the world. In every way, we focused on the Mexican education system historically, geopolitically and as a source of knowledge about it.

In this chapter, we focus on the time element in our understandings of the Mexican education system, and attempt to provide the contextual detail to how the system has changed and thus what it was first and how it functions now. In Chapter 2, we document the failures of sustainable reforms in the system over the last 100 years, and in effect contextualize system-wide reform efforts historically. Here, we begin the process of developing an argument about the nature of the Mexican system and inherent blockages to reforms within it. Chapter 3 focuses on curriculum and pedagogic reforms in the system. This chapter provides an illustration of how intended reforms are rarely able to overcome the blockages referred to earlier. Chapter 4 examines the training of teachers and administrators, pre-service and in-service education, including both official and independent initiatives, having established that the focus of any successful reform programme has to be on pedagogic practices and teachers' capacities to deliver them. This chapter provides a series of examples over time of the inability of the system to reform itself, and in particular in relation to developing its teacher workforce. Chapter 5 examines parental involvement in the system, for example, the Tizapán research 2010–13 and other official and independent initiatives, such as ACUDE. (This is the name given to the parental association 'Hacia una Cultura Democratica', operating in Mexico.) This chapter focuses on the role of parents and guardians in reform processes and suggests that their influence has been reduced by the structures in place and by an elite middle-class exodus from the state system. The focus in Chapter 6 is on alternative education programmes, and in particular, intercultural education. As with all the chapters in this book we contextualize these initiatives in relation to the history of the Mexican education system. In Chapter 7 we suggest that some reform and implementation processes are more successful than others, and these involve either working with the official system or working at its edges, and building constituencies and alliances with local, national and international partners. We conclude the book by looking in a more general and comparative sense at education reform processes and how they operate in socio-historical contexts.

History of the Mexican education system

The country of Mexico is located in the far southern part of the North American continent. It shares borders with the United States to the north, Guatemala, Belize and the Caribbean Sea to the south-east, the Gulf of Mexico to the east and the Pacific Ocean to the south and west. Encompassing roughly 760,000 square miles (2 million square kilometres), Mexico is the fifth largest country in the Americas by total area and the thirteenth largest independent nation in the world. Mexico has one of the world's largest economies; it is the tenth largest oil producer, the largest silver producer and is considered both a regional power and a middle-ranking power in the world. Additionally, Mexico was the first Latin American country to become a member of the Organisation for Economic Co-operation and Development (OECD) (since 1994), and is thought of as an upper-middle income country by the World Bank. It has the fourteenth largest nominal Gross Domestic Product (GDP) and the tenth largest GDP by purchasing power parity. The economy is strongly linked to those of its North American Free Trade Agreement (NAFTA) partners, especially the United States of America.

This federal republic is composed of 31 states and a federal district with a president, elected for a single six-year term, and a bicameral legislature. In 1921, a federal Secretariat of Public Education was created. Major changes occurred in Mexico in the years following the revolution and World War II, particularly the most extensive redistribution of land and fast industrialization. Schools were built throughout the country, providing greater educational opportunities for all Mexicans regardless of ethnicity or social class. This increase in educational opportunities coincided with a significant reduction in the infant mortality rate, which dropped from 222 deaths per 1,000 in 1920 to roughly 100 deaths per 1,000 by the mid 1940s.

It has largely been accepted by current historians and educationalists that the movement towards something approaching a national system of education has its roots in the endeavours of the generation of 'technocrats' who first argued for a national system. They flourished under the long dictatorship of Porfirio Díaz, who saw his mission as one of modernizing Mexico with his chief agent in the field of education being Justo Sierra Méndez. Ironically, the conception of the apparatus of the Mexican version of a modern state led to the creation and almost immediate expansion of a new middle class of administrators, managers and cadres dependent on the state and in personal terms for accumulating the cultural capital they required. Because the authoritarian nature of the state conflicted with their perceived needs and their ideology they provided the ideas and the impetus that initiated the Mexican Revolution that began in 1910 and culminated in José Vasconcelos in 1919 establishing a national system of education. There were two elements: firstly, the training of the administrative elite that was achieved by greatly expanding the system of *preparatorias* (upper secondary schools) and the refounding of the National University to serve those purposes; and secondly, the creation of a system of schooling whose main purpose was to assimilate the then vast rural population and ethnic minorities into society to minimize the possibility of civil strife. Hence, for the elite the *preparatorias* and the universities were designed to increase the cultural capital they required to occupy lifetime positions in government and administration, whilst the primary schools, which focused on maintaining social control, were designed to provide limited training for work and maximum training to accept the system that soon became known as the 'philanthropic ogre'(see Paz, 1994).

The system worked well until the late 1960s when it became apparent that at the upper levels of education there was an overproduction of students for the professions. This led to a largely student revolt by the sons and daughters of the *nomenklatura* that shook but did not open fatal fissures in the system. A greater challenge to the system was that by the 1980s Mexico was increasingly becoming an urban society with new demands for technical training and expertise. The harmony that existed between the political system and industry was shaken by the advent of Mexico's entry into the world economy. The system could no longer absorb the produce of the *preparatorias* and of the greatly expanded higher education institutions. Its implosion partially hid the contradiction in education between the need for social control that impedes creative and imaginative thinking and productive needs that require imagination and creativity. The advent of the 'war on drugs' in which over 100,000 have died so far and the growing unmasking of corruption at the heart of the political system and government agencies heightened the tension.

With the exception of Cuba, private education plays an important and increasing role in Latin American countries. In Mexico, there is a variety of private schools including those run by the Catholic Church, entrepreneurs and international organizations and agencies. The quality is very uneven and they are not regulated as carefully as the state system. Their growth coincides with the growth of a middle-class base. When the national system was small the public sector offered the possibility of such an accommodation. However, the move towards a mass education system led to a middle-class flight to private schools.

Because of its free trade agreement with the United States and Canada (NAFTA) and its entry into the Organisation for Economic Co-operation and Development (OECD) Mexico has become closely integrated into the global economy. The need for education has become even more important. From the end of the active phase of the Revolution in 1919 the country has exhibited a unique and unbroken commitment to education hallmarked by significant cultural achievements and the development of a dedicated group of educational researchers and practitioners. This continuity has been unique in Latin America. It has been underpinned by institutional continuity and a consistently high proportion of the budget devoted to educational provision, training and research. Research and innovatory programmes have been brought to life as a result of the government's promise to provide a modern system of education. This has evolved into a strong commitment to work with national and international institutions seeking to improve educational institutions and practices and to enhance the life chances of young people.

Despite these enormous efforts and a dedication to developing an education of quality, Mexico continues to languish at or near the bottom of every league table that measures educational achievement. The question therefore is how is this possible? In statistical terms, there are now about 26 million pupils in the system. Most attend part-time in multi-grade schools depending upon the individual state. A typical 15-year-old pupil will have had two years of preschooling, six years of primary schooling and three years of secondary education. This is known as basic education. The average school day extends to no more than four and a half hours, half that of South Korea and France. Only about half of the time spent in a school is devoted to learning as compared to the OECD average of 85 per cent. Analyses of the two major examinations purposefully designed to provide us with an indication of performance, ENLACE and PISA, indicate that the vast majority of pupils at age 15 have not attained the minimum level needed to find gainful employment. It is estimated that 38 per cent of the 15–19-year-old age group cannot read to an acceptable standard. Fully 79 per cent of that cohort cannot communicate in Spanish and about 80 per cent are deficient in mathematics. This may have declined even more over the last few years. Only 46 per cent of 15-year-old students enter upper secondary education. The dropout rate at this level is also increasing. Although education to the age of 18 is now obligatory, almost eight million pupils between the ages of 13 and 18 have left the system.

In order to understand the background to the reforms and the reforms themselves it is first of all necessary to have an understanding of the *de jure* and, more importantly, the *de facto* system of education and equally of the official and unofficial division of labour between stakeholders. The *de jure* education system is described as federal, consisting of 32 constituent state systems, enjoying a measure of financial and operational autonomy. However, finance is really controlled by the federal government, which must give its approval to local programmes before the funds are released; and state governments have little if any funds of their own to use. Operations are naturally constrained by finance. In part, the generation and development of programmes depends on the relative wealth of the states and whether they have the personnel to undertake such independent work. In basic education, the states are also bound to federal controls, a national curriculum and national systems of evaluation.

This *de facto* centralization is reinforced by corporate arrangements and practices that prevail through agreements between the federal administration (SEP) and the national teachers' union (SNTE) whose role since the imprisonment of its leader has reportedly been reduced. Until that time, promotions and transfers took place across and between the union and the administration. These arrangements had been sealed in a series of agreements and alliances, such as the most recent Alianza por la Calidad Educativa. This was mitigated at the state level if the SNTE was relatively independent of national headquarters or if more than one trade union existed in the state.

Despite important changes in the political structure over the last decade the system can still be characterized as being, in essence, corporative. That is, education is vertically integrated and tends to be inward looking and hierarchical. In human terms, it is held together by a complicated patchwork of individual and group loyalties across and upwards to the system. Loyalty is repaid with benefits, privileges and other concessions such as secondments, loans and transfers, that bind people to their superiors. It is not surprising then that educational considerations are frequently subsumed by political and personal considerations. In the Mexican political system, personal and political considerations are often one and the same. They count far more than policy considerations and often override ideological differences (see also Posner et al., 2017 for a fuller treatment of the issues we discuss in this and subsequent chapters, and Meyer, 1973).

The Mexican education system, corporative though it is, operates within a regionally diverse society. Ethnic, economic, social-class and geographical factors have played an important part in the development of the particularities of the state educational administration. For example, Aguascalientes and Colima are small and relatively well-endowed states with, in ethnic terms, a fairly homogenous population. Their administrations, including education, have benefited from these factors and their populations enjoy above average public services. Nuevo León is a relatively rich state with more resources than the norm and the neighbouring state of Coahuila is very much its satellite. At the other extreme, Chiapas, Guerrero, Nayarit, Oaxaca and Tabasco are states with high proportions of ethnically diverse people and high levels of poverty. Between these two extremes are the states of Jalisco, Sinaloa and Zacatecas in which coexist a large middle-class and urbanized population and specific regions of poverty, marginalization and ethnic minorities. In these states, as in Chiapas and Tabasco, the educational administrations struggle to meet the extremely varied needs of their people within their limited budgets. Yucatán with a long tradition of relative independence is one of the few states where an indigenous language is spoken across the state and has official recognition and also has resources that other states do not to ensure the survival of this language.

It can be argued that the root of the problem lies in educational institutions' clientelism, which means that successive governments of all political colours emphasize the politics of interpersonal and group loyalties over and above educational exigencies. The net result is poor planning and targeting, inappropriate use of resources and poor articulation between institutional and other stakeholders involved in education. Parents when they have the means attempt to avoid the state education system that, in their experience, seems incapable of improvement.

The population of Mexico is young, with a disproportionate number of students under the age of 25, and the school-age population doubling every six years or so. This has presented a number of problems in relation to the expansion of the schooling system. The solutions to those problems were radical, and involved using school facilities and teachers in two, and sometimes three, shifts in each day. Coping with the demands of this population expansion put considerable strain on the quality of the system. However, the continuous expansion may have helped to mask some of the systemic obstacles that make improvement in quality particularly difficult.

The rapid demographic growth slowed over the period up to the beginning of the twenty-first century. The school-age population increased between 2000 and 2015, as a result of government policy, when the length of compulsory schooling was extended, first in 2001 from nine to 11 years, and again in 2012 from 11 to 14 years, but the natural growth of the school age population ended around 2008. We will return to those policy-induced expansions in the school-age population later, but our analysis focuses in the first instance on this change from constant and rapid growth to zero growth, and the way in which this has brought to the fore the chronic question of quality, at the same time as making the condition acute.

So long as systems are growing, they hold out the prospect of self-correction. In much the same way as the problems of debt are automatically reduced in economies that are expanding, so poor quality can be addressed in expanding educational systems by improving the preparation of novice teachers. Poor quality teachers who are already in the system will reduce as a proportion of the whole educational workforce, and eventually retire. In education systems that have reached equilibrium, this focus on the initial preparation of teachers loses its potency as a policy for improving the quality of education as a whole. Attention has to be focused on the improvement of those teachers who are already in the system, as well as the facilities and environments that are provided by schools.

Some of the potential for reform of the system through growth was illusory in the case of Mexico, because, with teachers working double – and exceptionally triple – shifts, the absolute number of teachers was growing less rapidly than the number of students. However, before the 1990s the focus of educational reforms was on the initial preparation of teachers, with an extension of the length of training, an increase in the involvement of universities and equivalent institutions of higher education, and a raising of the level of teaching qualifications. This had been part of the move, noted across the world, to shift teaching towards an all-graduate profession and ensure the credibility of qualifications. This was promoted in Mexico by the establishment of the Universidad Pedagógica Nacional in 1978 (see also Rodríguez-Gómez, 2015). That emphasis on improving education through the pre-service preparation of teachers changed in 1993, when the government introduced the Carrera Magisterial as a way of improving the standard of teachers who were already in the system with a structured system of in-service training.

The Carrera Magisterial and the *Teaching Plaza*

The aim and purpose of the Carrera Magisterial was to offer incentives to practising teachers and to reward them for improving their qualifications and skills. Officially described as a system of horizontal promotion, the Carrera Magisterial was designed to overcome two problems, one generic to the teaching profession across the world, the other specific to the organization of the teaching profession in Mexico.

The Carrera Magisterial provided a system of horizontal promotion based on the skills and professional development of the teacher. There were 11 steps or stages, each of which was associated with a level of qualification, skill and engagement in continuing professional development, as well as providing a reward in terms of salary that was a fixed percentage of the basic teaching salary. Entry into the Carrera Magisterial was voluntary, and a teacher could only move from one step to the step immediately above in the scale. Assessment for that promotion involved a number of criteria, including seniority, qualifications, engagement in continuing professional development and the performance of students under the teacher's guidance.

In addition, the Carrera Magisterial included three strands that related to the role of the teacher in the education system. The first strand was for classroom teachers, while the other two strands were intended for those who carried more responsibility for the development of curricular materials and supporting learning, and for those who had more responsibility for the professional development of the personnel under their charge, respectively. Thus, teachers who achieved higher qualifications, who developed their skills and who could show that they had a positive impact on the learning of those in their care, were to be rewarded by promotion, with the intention that their professional status would be appropriately protected. The Constitution of Mexico and the General Law on Education specified that education was to be national, democratic, free and compulsory. Notwithstanding the specification that it would be national, many functions, including the implementation of the Carrera Magisterial were devolved to the individual states. This meant that implementation is heterogeneous, and that resources in different parts of the country were not equally allocated.

There were two major problems with the implementation of the Carrera Magisterial. The first is general to systems of professional development that rely on formal requirements, qualifications and certification; formal professional development is not always and necessarily mirrored in improved performance in the day-to-day tasks that face the professional. The second was more specific to the implementation of the Carrera Magisterial, in that insufficient resources were allocated to reward all of those who would otherwise have taken part.

By 2003 the cost of the augmented salaries associated with the programme was around 26 billion pesos. By that point there were teachers who had been promoted to each of the steps of the horizontal promotion scale. There was some hope that the system would become self-financing, as teachers retired from the upper levels at the same rate as new teachers joined at the lower levels. Around 2003 the system of horizontal promotion had become blocked, in much the same way as the system of vertical promotion had in 1993.

In order to understand the full import of the Carrera Magisterial, one needs to understand the concept of the plaza in Mexico. A dictionary definition of the word plaza is square (as in the Plaza Mayor in Mexico City), place or location, but there is also a sense in which it can be used to refer to position or teaching post. However, in this context the word carries much more force than that. Plaza, and the possession of a plaza, implies a sense of property ownership. In the first instance, plazas tended to be allocated to successful graduates of teacher training programmes. Most applicants who successfully completed a programme of initial teacher preparation received a plaza.

Of course, not all plazas were equal; plazas in attractive – normally urban – settings were highly prized, while plazas in remote rural locations were not. For the most part, plazas were allocated on the basis of merit, with the most attractive plazas going to those who achieved the highest marks, although some opportunity remained for that general schema to be modified by political and personal influences. There are two aspects to this placing of teachers and their geographical locations that arose from the application of this meritocratic principle. The first is that the most able teachers were concentrated in the most attractive regions, which particularly meant the urban and least impoverished areas. Those areas that were the most disadvantaged were allocated to those teachers who were less well qualified, and in this way cycles of deprivation were created.

The second aspect – which does not arise directly from the meritocratic principle, but from the paternalistic operation of the political structures in Mexico – is that those with political ambitions, and therefore political connections, can use those connections to their advantage, and particularly to stay close to the seat of political power in state capitals. Once allocated, however, the plaza had material status; it could be sold, bought, rented and even inherited. For example, a qualified teacher who did not wish to work in a rural area might buy a plaza in an urban area in order to make their work more congenial. Similarly, a family member might inherit a plaza from a deceased relative. Obviously, in all cases the new owner of the plaza must be a qualified teacher, but the link between performance and the desirability of the plaza, which was forged at the initial allocation of plazas, is rapidly eroded by the market operations that follow. This system of plazas was never universally applied, and even less so now because of the recent reforms to the system.

It is not difficult to see why the system of plazas is an impediment to the reform of the overall education system. Teachers regard their teaching position, not merely as personal property, but also a very real investment, which they may choose to realize at a later date. They have no reason to wish for, and every reason to oppose, a change that renders their investment worthless. As noted earlier, this obstacle to reform is even more constraining in a period of insignificant growth, when the rate of creation of new plazas is low, than it is in periods of high growth.

The Carrera Magisterial was abolished at the beginning of the current presidential administration (2013) and replaced first by an Examen Periódico Universal and then by open competition consisting of a multiple choice examination and evaluations by superiors supposedly based on the aspirant's quality of service. Plazas are now being phased out. Although the vast majority of teachers currently in service still hold plazas, they can be removed from service altogether if they fail an assessment or do not get assessed.

The political setting

The position of the unions is not always easily understood. The main political party in Mexico since the 1920s has been the Partido de la Revolución Mexicana (PRI), or Institutional Revolutionary Party. The PRI governed continuously between 1929 and 2000. The PRI was originally designed as the vehicle to institutionalize the socialist reforms of land ownership and labour that were the key outcomes of the revolution, which lasted from 1910 to 1920. However, the PRI has been pragmatic in its adoption of policies that would, in other circumstances, be described as left wing or right wing. Policies that would generally be seen as socialist (nationalization of resources, protectionism, state investment in infrastructure) or neoliberal (privatization of financial institutions, freedom on international trade, disruption of monopolies) have all been part of the PRI portfolio at one time or another.

In addition, after a continuous period of 71 years in power, the PRI, whose colours are red, white and green, the same as the Mexican flag, sometimes became so integrated with the organs of state that the boundaries between state and party become blurred, especially in rural areas. Similarly, the main teachers' union, which is affiliated with the PRI, is the Sindicato Nacional de Trabajadores de la Educación (SNTE) or National Union of Workers in Education. In the past, the PRI used public employees, among whom the teachers make up one of the largest groupings, to stage public demonstrations of support for the party/government (over the very long time when the two were more or less synonymous). In return, the union was rewarded with concessions that included the maintenance of such restrictive practices as the system of plazas.

The close relationship between the PRI and the SNTE came under increasing strain, and matters came to a head in 1989, when the President of the Sindicato Nacional de Trabajadores de la Educación (SNTE), Carlos Jonguitud Barrios, was forced from power by the President of the Republic, Carlos Salinas de Gortari. He was succeeded as President of the Union by Elba Esther Gordillo Morales, who has subsequently been imprisoned on charges of appropriation of union funds, money laundering and criminal activity in 2013. The exact causes of this turbulence in the union are, of course, shrouded in the mists of time, but it is clear that, at the very least, the union has lost some of the protection of the PRI that it once enjoyed. It is interesting to note that the division between the SNTE and the PRI became increasingly acrimonious as the growth of the education system slowed, and the need to reform the system, and especially that of plazas, became more pressing.

Roberto Rodríguez-Gómez (2015) has examined the complex history of the relationship between the Secretaria de Educación Pública and the unions. The changing context, especially the decentralization of education to the individual states, meant that the SNTE increased its power through a process of double negotiation in which the union negotiated at both the national and the local levels. After an interregnum of 12 years, the PRI regained supreme power in the country when Enrique Peña Nieto was elected President of Mexico in 2012. Peña Nieto has made the reform of the education system one of the central planks of his platform as president, and has proposed substantial changes in the terms and conditions of work of teachers. In this he is supported by the SNTE, but opposed by the Coordinadora Nacional de Trabajadores de la Educación (CNTE) or National Coordinating Committee of Workers in Education. This breakaway union, which is strongest in Oaxaca and several other southern states, opposes the reform, and especially that of the system of plazas. Rubén Nuñez, leader of the Oaxaca chapter of the union, is reported to have asserted that '(t)hey will not take what is ours', using language that underlines the point made earlier, that teachers have come to see themselves as having property rights over their plaza (*Financial Times*, 22 July 2015).

The links between political stances and the underlying problems of the education system are not always clearly delineated. However, Oaxaca has approximately the same school population as the state of Michoacán, but the former has twice as many teachers (*Financial Times*, 22 July 2015). In addition, the State Institute of Public Education of Oaxaca (IEEPO) is staffed by 4,000 teachers who, as well as the salaries that they draw at the institute, also have plazas from which they also derive an income. It is estimated that the institute could run efficiently with a staff of 500 (see also *Financial Times*, 22 July 2015). But identifying causal relationships is more difficult, and it is not clear whether the inefficiency in Oaxaca arises from the strength of the union, or whether the union is strong because more vested interests are involved.

This political conflict was exacerbated in 2015. It may be that the extensions of the length of compulsory schooling in 2001 and 2012 were an attempt to postpone the problem in the appointment and promotion systems by creating artificial growth in the education system. Such measures were only temporary, however, and in 2015 President Peña Nieto, with some hesitation, supported a more lasting reform of the education system (see also *Financial Times*, 2 June 2015). It should perhaps be noted, however, that the reforms of 2015 did not arise out of nowhere. In 2006 the Secretaria de Educación Pública introduced the Evaluación Nacional del Logro Académico en Centros Escolares (National Evaluation of Academic Achievement in Educational Centres) (ENLACE). This was an attempt to evaluate the performance of teachers by assessing the performance of their students. Given the cycles of deprivation that have been noted earlier, with the less qualified teachers going to the more deprived areas, this points to the potential unfairness of evaluating teachers in this way. However, Rodríguez-Gómez (2015) notes other serious shortcomings of the ENLACE, in particular the fact that the level of aggregation of the results meant that it was impossible to use these as an indicator of the quality of any particular teacher or educational institution. As a result, ENLACE was not of value as a tool for the improvement of the system.

The General Law of Service in the Teaching Profession (Ley General del Servicio Profesional Docente (LGSPD)) was passed in September 2013 (Government of Mexico, 2013). Details of the programme that was to replace the Carrera Magisterial were published in May 2015 (Coordinación Nacional del Servicio Profesional Docente (CNSPD). The CNTE has maintained its protests against the reforms since the publication of the General Law (LGSPD) in 2013, but the political stakes have been raised as the government has shown its determination to push forward with the reforms in 2015. It therefore makes sense to think of these as the reforms of 2015, even though, technically, the relevant legal framework was set up in 2013.

Article 2 of the LGSPD sets out the four objectives of the law: to regulate the service provided by the teaching profession at all levels of education up to the *bachillerato* or equivalent; to establish standards, measures and indicators for use in the teaching profession; to establish the rights and obligations of those engaged in the teaching profession and to ensure transparency and accountability in the teaching profession. Article 21 sets out the requirements for entry into the profession, namely that there are open procedures for appointment to positions on the basis of annual competitions, where all the details of the criteria and procedures are to be published in advance. Such procedures have to be approved by the Secretary of Education. In addition, Article 23 sets out constraints on the appointment of individuals to positions that fall vacant in the course of an academic year. Generally speaking, those appointed should be those who took part in the previous open competition, but who failed to secure a position, starting with the best qualified. But, in any event, such interim appointments are temporary, and subject to review and confirmation at the end of the academic year in which they take place.

Article 22 introduces an induction period of two years for new teachers, during which they will have an appointed mentor to oversee their professional development. This induction period includes two very important hurdles before the teacher can be confirmed in a permanent post: they must complete the first six months of employment without unfavourable reports, and they must pass an evaluation at the end of the first year. As a result of that evaluation, the new teacher may be required to attend a specified professional development programme. Failure to attend, or to obtain a satisfactory evaluation, can result in dismissal from the teaching service.

Taken together, although the question of the sale of plazas and other restrictive practices is not directly mentioned in the law, the implementation of these measures would effectively mean an end to the idea that a plaza is an object that can be owned, or its ownership transferred in a commercial transaction. This is the official purpose of these measures that are specified in the LGSPD. Only days before the enactment of the LGSPD, the Senate of the Republic (2013, 1) issued a proclamation that included the following:

> In the processes for appointment of teachers to initial positions, and in subsequent promotions to senior positions, there have predominated, over many years, criteria which have nothing to do with academic work, or with the skills and capabilities that are necessary to discharge the duties of teacher, such as influence and nepotism, even including passing positions to relatives, or the sale of teaching posts.

The system of professional development that was incorporated in the Carrera Magisterial was voluntary, but has been replaced by a system that carries sanctions for those who are unable or unwilling to meet the standards set by the responsible national authorities. In the next chapter, we consider the specific difficulties with reforming the system.

2
Reforming the System: Successes and Failures

So far in our account of the Mexican education system reforms we have highlighted the repeated failures of the Mexican government to implement meaningful and sustainable system-wide reforms despite sometimes comprehensive and well-prepared programmes to improve curriculum, pedagogy and evaluation. It is important to stress that from the outset the Mexican system was organized in a top-down fashion. It was created entirely by the state rather than by social pressure from large swathes of the population as happened in Europe. In our attempt to identify the possible causes for these tenaciously persistent blockages and the poor performance of the system we must start with this key idea.

Let us be clear at the outset. The current crisis in Mexican education is not only the failure to put into effect a new set of curricular, pedagogic and evaluation reforms, but also the continued myopia to learn from the past. The impediment to educational change is often not the 'why' and the 'what' but the 'how'. Locating the underlying reasons for this continuing failure requires a knowledge of schools and educational stakeholders and their relationship to the social balance of power. In particular, the idiosyncratic non-entrepreneurial Mexican middle class that, as we will see, is largely both the product and the defender of the Mexican state configuration, and is very different from that of European and Anglo-Saxon countries. However, this aspect has been barely raised by academics and never enters the collective mind of the various generations of so-called reformers. The reformers tend to concentrate on the relatively safe areas of the 'why' and the 'what' of education. That is, more deeply and less considered is the idea that it requires an understanding of the social forces that constitute and maintain particular configurations of educational institutions and their practices if a coherent strategy for reform is to be developed.

For those reasons, it is of paramount importance for us to understand the origins and itinerary of those systems of education that are state-created, as is the case in Mexico, rather than resulting from alliances of disparate social groups as was the case in most of Europe. Since the eclipse of what we can call the conceptually oriented sociology of education developed by researchers as different in their origins and destinations as Émile Durkheim, Max Weber, Basil Bernstein, Pierre Bourdieu, more historically inclined researchers such as Maurice Halbwachs and more recently Margaret Archer, the field has been occupied by instrumental and pragmatic observers who attempt to construe systems and practices without any real understanding of and reference to the structures of those societies. This has led to a culture of context-free proposals and plans sponsored to a large extent by even more remote international institutions. The continual failure of the process of reform leads to a devaluation of these efforts and contributes in no small way to the alienation of significant social groups from the process of construction and development.

Therefore, our aim is to examine the specificity, the uniqueness and the lessons to be drawn from a socio-historical analysis of the development and current structure of Mexico's system of education. However, before we can present a reasonable chronology it is important to point out that it must be contextualized by an understanding of the nature of Mexican society that allows the generation of programmes and institutions in some cases and hinders or makes it impossible in others. That is, the social purpose and function of the education system must be examined before we look at the evolution of its institutions and practices. In a previous work (Scott et al., 2012) we suggested that unless there is a firm, coherent sustainable and viable system for the implementation of plans, programmes and what are usually called reforms, there is little chance that even those ideas drawn from the best of home and international practices can be translated into progressive mechanisms, let alone changes in the classroom.

We have two major problems here: the lack of research into implementation, that is, the translation of ideas into action, and related to it a misunderstanding of obstacles in the path of change and progress. This is complemented by the idea that the terminology of reform and of implementation to the extent that it is used is not sufficiently society specific. Here we have a problem of terminology that affects how the process has been contextualized. The interjection of concepts derived from attempts to understand European societies unfortunately does not help because their relevance to Mexican society is questionable. Indeed, some of these concepts have strong political undertones and render an attempt at analysis not only far too functional but also judgemental. A key term here, as we will see, is corruption, often used in the Mexican context to describe and/or excuse the supposedly anomalous development of educational institutions and their deviation from the accepted norms that have become the yardstick of international organizations like the OECD. However, before exploring this area it is important to reflect upon the lack of sufficiently grounded research into educational institutions and processes of implementation.

The lack of research and information

Mexican institutions have traditionally strongly discouraged fundamental criticism of those academic and research activities into how the system responsible for management and implementation functions, because it is widely perceived that such research could undermine its authority. This leads to a disjuncture between theory and research that, for our purposes, means that there is very little firm empirical information to help us construct an analysis of the system and its effects on educational institutions and practices.

The irony at the root of the lack of information stems from the fact that those who normally would analyse and comment on the development of educational institutions and practices were and continue to be part of the system itself. To varying degrees, they were the authors and beneficiaries of the corporative system that fostered such a group in order to guarantee its survival institutionally and intellectually, as well as of the development and refinement of the instruments of social control and social selection. Indeed, it can be argued that this group itself was largely the creation of the post-1917 social and political consensus, as Enrique Krauze (1976) suggests in his studies of the Mexican intellectual elite which emerged from the revolution, and was directly and indirectly so beholden to the state that a fundamental critique of that state was impossible. Whilst part of their social apprenticeship would have involved criticism of the system, their eventual co-option into the system reduced their opposition to it.

Firstly, very little empirical work concerning education and educability was conducted through agencies close to government institutions and their ancillary bodies largely because the system, in part, guaranteed its survival by a disjuncture between the word (the revolutionary rhetoric of the active phase of the Mexican Revolution 1910–17 which became the moral basis for the nationalistic consensus) and the deed (the actual networking activities of the closely interrelated state and private institutions). Even when studies concerning the failure of education to deliver were carried out they were never made public.

Secondly, this meant that the intellectual elites were attracted to theoretical constructs that both granted them academic accolades and which were not dangerous to the established consensus. This could explain, in part, the tendency to collect theories from abroad that would never be applied successfully to the reality of Mexico. The disjuncture between theories and reality meant that such theories could never be used to describe the nature of Mexican society; nor more importantly, could they provide the launching pad for theories that would contribute to social and educational change. That is, in the Mexican context the Fabian and the social reformist tradition in the field of education, that is, the strategy pioneered by A. H. Halsey et al. (1980) in Britain, was almost totally absent.

There were, however, a few notable exceptions found on the margins of social enquiry, largely through institutions financed by progressive Catholic and international organizations that congregated around such organizations as the Centro de Estudios Educativos (CEE) and its offshoots. However, the essence of such groups was that they dedicated themselves to working with marginal social groups that the corporativist system found impossible to deal with and they were further marginalized by mainstream academia largely on the grounds that they lacked a coherent theoretical base.

In this chapter, we focus on the agents and agencies responsible for the establishment of educational institutions and practices, their modifications and perfecting of the system and their reactions to the incorporation of Mexico into local and international agreements, which was, in effect, to lead to a crisis that undermined their work. However, in order to do so it is necessary to highlight some significant differences not only in the way the relationship between education and agencies and agents of social and political control are constituted in Mexico but also to stress that what is regarded as normal practices within the Western European and Anglo-Saxon tradition(s) are not applicable to the Mexican experience.

Were we to start with the premise that the overriding purpose of any system and practice of education in a hierarchical society is selection and control, we would quickly have to add that the relative weights of these two elements varies according to the structure of the social polity. Societies in which economic competition is stressed tend to put more weight, at least formally, on open competition. Here the organization of educational systems both materially and symbolically is relatively open and the modalities of control are weak. On the other hand, societies in which the maintenance of social order is of paramount concern are more likely to attempt to use educational systems and practices that both materially and symbolically place greater emphasis on control. This obviously has an effect on agents, their perceptions and practices as well as conditioning the way research is and can be conducted. On the whole, European countries have practised the former, with variations due to the periodic strength of oppositional forces and a complex and changing system of social alliances with the largely professional middle class often in alliance with working-class organizations. The history of Mexico from its political revolution of 1910 until recent times is an example of a system and practice of education which emphasizes control and in which the bulk of the middle class never enjoyed an independent status, being beholden to the system itself for its continued existence. Hence, the non-entrepreneurial Mexican middle class was never in a position to translate control into power and was never able to forge alliances with oppositional groups.

Key problems and concepts

It is important to give an account of the state of education that prevailed prior to the advent of the modern Mexican state. Until the 1880s it is difficult to speak of Mexican society in the same way as one does of a European society. Mexican independence was achieved through the successful actions of a dissident army faction in conjunction with the power of landed interests, and these groups spent the better part of a century in a civil war and in opposition to the increasing influence of emerging urban groups. The division was so great that not only could national institutions not be firmly established but also almost half of Mexico's territory was seized by the United States. The only national organizations were the armies, tiny by modern standards, with generals in the role of what has been called 'slash and burn' politics. From the 1880s schools were established but only in urban areas where they reached a small percentage of the population. The continuity between pre-revolutionary education policies and those developed by the new authorities is probably greater than has been stressed in the literature. When José Vasconcelos began his work in the National University and later as the first Minister of Education, he already found an existing network of schools and programmes.

Secondary and higher education were largely concerned with producing administrators and only became involved in professional training in the second half of the twentieth century. In the provinces an embryonic non-entrepreneurial middle class, largely composed of professionals, attempted to set up their own institutions for professional training. These institutions that adopted a positivistic ideology were subject to chaotic openings and closures due to outside political pressures. There was no national system of education as one would expect of a nation that at this time was territorial rather than cultural, nor until the 1880s with the formation of a group called the 'Científicos', of which Justo Sierra Méndez was the spokesperson, do we find attempts to create what Emile Durkheim ([1895] (1982)) called 'a collective consciousness'. As Patricia de Leonardo (1983) points out, no single group or force was powerful enough to establish its hegemony and hence build a national system of schooling. However, each was powerful enough to dismantle whatever their opponents set up during their fleeting moments of power. The quasi-dictatorial regime headed by Porfirio Díaz (1876–1911) made moves towards the establishment of a state and in its later years towards the development of practices inspired by the idea of mechanical solidarity but its conflict with foreign interests and its inability to satisfy emerging urban society led to its demise through a series of internal civil wars.

Mexican corporative society

As previously suggested, the social structure and the history of Mexican society is fundamentally different in origin and its current structure from those of, for example, the United Kingdom, France or Germany. These societies function as relatively liberal capitalist societies where conflict has been reduced to operations within what have become established and accepted political institutions. In these societies, there is a unitary system for the distribution of material and symbolic values based upon a general consensus that underlies the legitimation of these institutions. In order to understand Mexican society, it is important to put to one side assumptions that stem from that social settlement, and examine more closely the relationship between social groups in Mexico. Only then can we discuss allocation mechanisms and understand how they function in the realm of education.

If this is true of the agencies it is equally true of the agents. The descriptive terms, middle class, working class and so forth have precise meanings within metropolitan contexts. These meanings are derived from the complex relationship between social groups that generate the agencies and can modify or even eliminate them. The terms cannot be applied to Mexican society without first being contextualized by the very different and equally complex relationship between social groups in that society.

The wealth of this middle segment of society has little to do with physical capital. Because of their training and position in society they are vocal and also can be creative. Their property, that is, cultural capital, is their ability to manage and control. This segment of the middle class is composed of a body of specialized agents with specific interests and specific educational needs. Like traditional shamans as described by the structural anthropologists, their role, in part, is the concealment of domination through hidden rules regarding the generation of material and symbolic values. In terms of functions, this new middle class is composed of regulators, repairers, diffusers, shapers and executors. In terms of social reproduction, they require a rigorous system of professionalization through education. Hence, the middle class, as a whole, is both the beneficiary and author of the education system, and recent ideological conflicts over education are characterized as resulting from the differing views of the commercial and the professional middle classes. Therefore, if we suggest that the principal means for allocation within Mexican society is *corruption*, we imply something very different from the term used every day within metropolitan societies; the very term that metropolitan political sociology has found impossible to translate into an analytical tool for understanding Mexican society.

What do we mean when we say that corruption is the heart and essence of Mexican society? Here our starting point must be a review of what is meant by a corporativist society. Whilst generally working within a capitalist framework, corporativist systems are largely governed by centralized institutions where social, political and economic power is shared out among the elites of various and sometimes competing groups, none of which can obtain hegemony over the others on their own. The alliances – if one can use that term to describe an uneasy system based on mutual suspicion – are usually unstable and have been held together and continue to be maintained by what can be best described as mutual defence pacts. An intricate system of checks and balances is repeated within every governmental institution from the top to the lower positions. This means that any reform or suggested innovation has to be so rigorously examined that often it does not survive the process of scrutiny. Hence, to the evident chagrin of international banks and their associated agencies, purely economic aims are ultimately sacrificed to the aim of maintaining social cohesion; as are education aims. Indeed, the process of educational reform is made all the more difficult because although major stakeholders have some kind of representation within the ministry, the outside agencies nonetheless still reserve, as we will see, the right to intervene in the process. In extreme cases they take to the streets to oppose a process, innovation or reform to which they are formally committed.

Whilst in the economic sphere private enterprises are often dominant within the processes of decision making and, indeed, members of the same family act from outside and inside the ministry, many of their aims are consciously attenuated and, indeed, sacrificed in order to maintain social order. That is, at best the system is based on compromises worked out by the elites of the hitherto competing sectors who congeal into an elite of their own. This elite has, in recent times, expanded greatly and has, in some cases, developed its own agenda.

The weakness of the Mexican version of such a socio-political arrangement is that it is based upon mutual suspicion and, for this new and highly educated elite, that it thwarts the achievement of its own desired ends in order to avoid challenge and conflict. However, this new managerial elite develops its own norms, rules and systems of social promotion that can come into conflict even with its sponsoring organizations. Promotion is achieved not through merit but through networking usually funnelled through a single agency like a political organization and its ancillaries. Each elite distributes positions through its ranks based upon service to that elite or the overall system. In liberal democratic societies with precise rules and regulations for promotion, this fundamentally different system of distribution is generally called corruption.

Hence, a corporativist system of social and political control relies on the networking established by co-option and sometimes especially created social groups. Networking usually refers to the complex system of rewards and processes of mutual help and promotion within family units and political units. Claudio Lomnitz (2000) used the term to describe the survival of marginal social groups and it can be extended to encompass the complex system of relations between groups whose first priority is an avoidance of conflict. This involves sacrificing immediate interests for a complicated process of negotiation and reward, which has little to do with talent as defined through the theory of human capital or a notion of merit based upon competence rather than performance.

The role of organizing and maintaining a central system of values and what we can call the social controllers whose shaman-like task it is to oversee those processes is very much more important than in liberal democratic societies, because the institutions they control are necessarily of greater importance and extend to areas such as culture that the political institutions of liberal democratic societies do not touch. In such a society, more stress is therefore placed upon education as a controlling rather than an allocation device and its systems of curriculum, pedagogy and evaluation are vitiated by messages of the need to operate within the acceptable framework. It is also important to note that whilst a corporativist structure seems to be stable, that stability is not necessarily as immutable as it might seem. A corporativist configuration is successful only so long as the main and overriding priority is social order. Once that priority changes, or is perceived to have changed, the delicate alliance that by nature restricts the aspirations of the participating social groups may unravel.

A comparison between corporativist systems is difficult because there are few examples of such systems lasting for more than a relatively short period of time and the nature of those systems varies because of the structure of the societies for and in which they have been created. We will see that this was the basis of the Mexican state that emerged from the chaotic revolutionary period that began in 1910 when the established society imploded. We will also see that since the opening up of Mexico, the hallmark of which was the NAFTA agreement that came into effect in 1994, and the enormous influence of the millions of Mexicans and their families who emigrated to the United States whilst retaining significant links in the country of their origin, this has been somewhat, but perhaps less than one has imagined, attenuated.

Another term that requires definition is that which characterizes the agent managing the search for and the maintenance of a social consensus, that is, the middle class, which takes a particular form in Mexico. We must be careful using the concept of social class in the Mexican context. Not only is the concept socially specific but also dependent upon the relative homogeneity of the relations of production within a social entity and to date, despite many interesting explorations, we still do not possess a general term that helps us to understand the nature of Mexican society. For our immediate purpose the definition of social class we are using is a modification of that used by Basil Bernstein (1998). Social classes and relations between them are constituted by and also constitute inequalities in the distribution of material and symbolic power. These are derived from and realized through the creation, organization, distribution, legitimation and reproduction of both the material and symbolic values arising out of the prevailing social division of labour of which they are a part.

Whilst there has been in Mexico since the late nineteenth century a small urban bourgeoisie engaged in business and commerce, yet far larger and far more important has been that social group who conceive of themselves as a middle class but are largely professional in nature, surviving by an accumulation of cultural rather than economic capital. It is a group whose principal role has been the running of institutions. It is not 'middle class' as an intermediary between an aristocracy and peasantry or proletariat, as in nineteenth-century France, but a middle class which is the agent of a small office-holding power elite (largely recruited from themselves) who constitute the state apparatus. Every different formation of the middle class in the modern world has, of all the social groups, incorporated the most directly perceivable interest and role in education both in terms of social control and of its own perpetuation. But each middle class is conditioned by different socio-historical and political settings of which the Mexican is one of the most distinctive. Certainly, this Mexican middle class is the group least studied, an irony in itself since from the very beginning of the social sciences most of its practitioners are themselves from this very social group.

In a sense, it is no exaggeration to argue that the history of educational systems and practices in corporativist societies is the autobiography of its agent, the middle class. This can be readily seen in Mexico because the middle class was created largely by the corporativist state and schizophrenically, both supported that consensus whilst seeking to escape its embrace. Its adventures with the Socialist Education Movement of the 1930s, whilst seeking to educate its children in schools free from such an ideology; its institutional support of the secularization of education, whilst privately remaining Catholic; and its founding and then abandonment of state universities and polytechnics for private institutions, are part of our exploration.

The constitution of the hegemony (1917–34)

The history of modern Mexico, as something more than just the territorial entity inherited from the Spanish crown, began with what has been characterized as the Mexican Revolution that exploded with great violence in 1910. The founding of the extremely efficient agency of social control, social consensus and distributor of material and symbolic values, the Partido Nacional Revolucionario (PNR), was initiated in 1929 by one of the principal architects of the new social order, Plutarco Elías Calles. It was transformed in 1938 by General Lázaro Cárdenas del Río into the more functional Partido de la Revolución Mexicana (PRM), and then sanctified appropriately by the more industrially minded Miguel Alemán Valdés, who had overseen the creation of the party machine and cemented its links with the industrial elite as the Partido de la Revolución Mexicana (the Institutional Revolutionary Party or PRI) in 1946. The history of Mexico can be best characterized as an irresolvable battle between social forces each too weak and isolated to establish a lasting hegemony, yet strong enough to prevent other groups or coalitions from maintaining power for any significant period of time.

The shock of the bloody revolutionary civil war (1910–17) during which time approximately 1 million out of a population of 17 million died as a result of regional wars and civil wars within civil wars led to a forced settlement brokered by a group of army officers led by Álvaro Obregón Salido (1880–1928). Like Elías Calles, many of the founders of the party had started their working lives as schoolteachers who saw their role as one of creating a cohesive and stable civil society and seeking where possible conciliation and equal rights. The exhausted participants, peasant organizations, nascent working-class organizations, local potentates and a small entrepreneurial and even smaller professional middle class could only agree to what in a very real sense was a 'shotgun marriage'. The best depiction of this period is found not in a social science textbook but in the satirical novel by Jorge Ibargüengoitia Antillón, *Los Relámpagos de Agosto* (1964), that parodied the memories of the veterans of the 1910 Revolution and how by shifting from physical to economic warfare they reaped immense and lasting benefits. The authorities accepted the satire of their history whilst also effectively banning the all too realistic and unsanitized early historical study of Jean Meyer (1973) called *La Revolución Mexicana*.

The first phase of the development of the modern state under the post-revolution presidents, Álvaro Obregón (1920–24) and Plutarco Elías Calles (1924–8) and Calles' surrogates who served until 1934, was mainly a political phase that consisted in laying the foundations of the political and economic institutions necessary to guarantee social peace. They used the already existing mechanism of the state to mould existing institutions and to create new ones that had a triple function: to maintain social order; to serve as bodies that would absorb the various social groups capable of upsetting that order; and to provide the economic and social accoutrements of a modern state through these institutions.

Parallel to and overlapping with the state was a series of political movements that Calles succeeded in moulding into an institution that in theory represented all social classes and groups through a process of institutionalization.

Secondly, the various disparate groups that had participated in the revolution had to be incorporated into some form of consensus. The army had to be converted into administrators and businessmen. The trade unions in urban centres had to be transformed into institutions responsive to the state and a middle class had to be created or reoriented to administer these and the ancillary organizations, the basic components of a modern state. Until the advent of the Obregón–Calles regime, little real attention had been given to education below the level of higher education. It was quickly realized that a national system was required to mould the territory into a nation state and intellectuals like Vasconcelos laid the bases for an ideology best characterized as a vigorous Durkheimian form of consensus. The teacher, particularly in rural areas where practically no schooling existed, was regarded as an educational missionary, a heroic purveyor of knowledge and civilization in the form of a fierce Mexican nationalism based on a mythical history that included the Aztecs, Benito Juárez and the 1910 revolutionaries. The first group of cultural missionaries was created in 1921 but the movement was only consolidated in 1923. The teachers were seen as agents of the state and, during the revolt of peasant communities known as the Cristiada in the late 1920s, many were assassinated.

The institutions established by Obregón were refined by Calles and his surrogates, in collaboration with Calles' right-hand man, the pedagogue, Moisés Sáenz. Upon the assassination of Obregón in 1928, Calles skilfully replaced the reliance on a single figure, 'the caudillo', with a complex system based upon an all-inclusive party strongly articulated with both private economic institutions and a state apparatus strong enough not to collapse with the disappearance of its leading figures. The corporative party thus emerged as the representative of what Calles characterized as the active and leading groups of society: the army, the peasantry, the urban workers and the popular classes. Each group functioned as an aggregator of the demands and responsibilities of its constituency as well as negotiating through the party the appropriation of various sectors of the federal and state administrations that became their respective fiefdoms. After a period of time, the army, whose leaders were effectively transformed into administrators and/or entrepreneurs or simply eliminated, as beautifully described by Jorge Ibargüengoitia in his satirical novels, lost its *raison d'être* as one of the governing sectors, which was henceforth reduced to a trinity. The other groups were effectively bureaucratized and the state organizations, with the possible partial exception of the Ministry of Education, became organizations for the necessary distribution of patronage without which the system could not function. Positions were awarded through networking that sometimes was equivalent to merit, but which was the key to social advancement and maintaining social order.

They, in turn, organized themselves in paternalistic and corporativist ways. In part, the conversion from the earlier overwhelming agrarian economy in which the need for middle-class professionals, that is, a middle class based on the accumulation of cultural rather than physical capital, its related expansion of urban centres from market towns and military barracks and the beginning of the long era of rapid demographic growth, matched the need for professionals, administrators and for what Julien Benda (1927) called *les clercs*. The system's need for institutions to train this new middle class paralleled the needs of these greatly expanded and articulated groups. It was a perfect match that satisfied both the system and those who populated the system until such a time when supply and demand could no longer be matched and the pull of human capital theory was no longer so compelling.

That is, something like a modern state apparatus was needed. This, in turn, required appropriate agencies and agents capable of training those to run such institutions. Under José Vasconcelos Calderón, called the 'cultural caudillo' of the Mexican Revolution and later to be the first Minister of Education (1921–3), the National University was re-established with the new purpose of training a generation of professionals beholden to the state and not to the Roman Catholic Church. The modernization and establishment of a system of state universities followed this reconstitution of the National University. Indeed, Vasconcelos, as both rector and minister, was the key figure in imbuing the new education with what he called a civilizing and spiritual ethos. This was reflected in the often-heroic campaigns to reduce illiteracy and the first efforts to establish a system of rural education which itself had the intention of promoting national unity through programmes with a strong dose of nationalism and scientific progress combined.

Indeed, almost every document produced by the government saw the Secretaría de Educación Pública as the most important catalyst for establishing national identity and reinforcing the state as the organization par excellence to achieve and preserve social harmony. What was never stated, of course, was that the system could be used to absorb large sections of the new middle class and the aspiring peasantry, providing not only jobs for each other but also solid consensual institutions.

The consolidation of the hegemony (1934–45)

Land reform that had never been a high priority of Calles was central to the programme of Lázaro Cárdenas, who occupied the presidency from 1934–40. His period of office not only promoted the redistribution of land and the setting of limits on landholdings but also the organization of a semi-system of collective property called the ejido. In theory, the land within an ejido was collectively owned but in practice the manager, who also doubled as a party official, ran the organization, sometimes resorting to less than agreeable sanctions. Parallel to the organization of the ejido was the extension of party control to rural areas where the majority of the population still lived, and it was difficult to sometimes distinguish between party and ejido control.

Whilst very little was provided in terms of educational programmes for the newly enfranchised smallholders, the extension of educational institutions to the countryside was also a priority of the regime. The programme, called the Socialist Education Movement, was staffed by thousands of young and often untrained teachers who envisaged a radically new society – with some modelling their ideas on what they assumed must be taking place in the Soviet Union. There was no real socialist content to the educational project and usually no curriculum and pedagogy suitable to stimulating production in the countryside. There were exceptions in terms of maverick and dedicated teachers, but, as we will see, they too were brought under control by the development of a teachers' trade union that was created to be part of the institutions designed to secure and maintain social control. Socialism in the Mexican context was defined as educating human beings supposedly free of prejudices and religious fanaticism (a violent civil war having been fought by proponents and opponents of the Church during the late 1920s and early 1930s), and a supposedly egalitarian society propelled by a romantic and inspiring vision. Here we find the first instance of a revolutionary rhetoric being skilfully used to promote a reality that was far from egalitarian. At this time, most young people still did not have access to schools, few teachers were sufficiently trained and schools were often fleetingly present institutions.

The schools, to the extent that they existed, had the purpose of communicating the moral basis of the society and determining that the population accepted government institutions as defenders of the new order and therefore inviolate to criticism. The moral basis of that order and the refinement of the institutions and party was the work of Calles' elected successor, student and later nemesis, Lázaro Cárdenas. Once the institutional basis for the state was in place and the army organized with civilian lines of command, Cárdenas' task was to organize the institutions for the purposes of achieving a social consensus, and lay the basis for a national system of education. The moral basis of this agreed programme was established through the foundation of specialized institutions, such as what was to become the Colegio de México, charged with the devising of a justificatory history and a curriculum for the school system, the Instituto Politecnico Nacional to train engineers and administrators and special colleges established to train a generation of teachers within the national ideology initially and confusingly called 'socialist education'. These institutions and their articulation with state and quasi-state bodies on an official level, and with private organizations through family networking on the more important unofficial level, provided not only social mobility for the existing middle classes but also laid the basis for the creation of a state-dependent middle class, which was also to provide the backbone of the party institutions.

The already established middle class that had lived through the destruction of its physical capital during the 'Bloody Decade' saw the emerging corporativist state as an insurance policy and its quasi-state institutions as providing scope for their reaccumulation of capital. A large segment eagerly embraced the opportunities newly provided by the corporativist state as an alternative to the acquisition of physical capital and earnestly promoted the development of educational institutions and practices which, to as great an extent as possible, would allow them to develop those skills. The generation of intellectuals who like Vasconcelos had supported the earlier radical phase of the revolution became strong proponents of the national consensus, the authors of its texts and, in some cases, its friendly critics. Often families like those of Antonio Caso, Daniel Cosío Villegas, Manuel Gómez Morín, Alfonso Reyes, Aaron and Moisés Saénz and Jesús Silva Herzog operated like diversified corporations working both in and between state and private institutions. Either that or they devised, like many others, a division of labour, in which some were in the private sector, others in the state sector, others in institutions like the university, but all united in what outsiders would probably want to classify as a family firm. The model was perfected after 1946 by Miguel Alemán Valdés who reformulated the public–private partnership and with the help of Torres Bodet, removed the more overtly ideological references from the project, dispensing with socialist rhetoric and replacing it with a more developmentalist ideology.

However, in terms of education, there was an important tension. Firstly, the middle class required a system of education, particularly at the higher level, which would guarantee that their offspring would be able to rise to similar positions. Secondly, they required a system of education that would allow for a modest increase in the production of professionals to manage the system through an expansion of secondary and then higher education. Thirdly, they required a system and practices of education that would create and maintain a national consensus.

The apogee of the hegemony (1945–68)

After 1945 the national consensus was so firmly rooted in the collective consciousness that the trappings of the socialist ideology could be replaced by another. This was in line with a purely economistic model of development and widely shared view that Mexico must industrialize, with the newly reconstituted PRI substituting for Adam Smith's invisible hand. During his two long periods as Secretary of Education, Jamie Mario Torres Bodet (1943–6 and 1958–64) laid the foundations for a system of education that vitiated the society and played an important role in the organization of teachers' groups into a single trade union, the Sindicato Nacional de Trabajadores de la Educación (SNTE). The state through the ever-expanding Ministry of Education became the sole source of research and finance for the development of educational programmes and policies. From the time of Torres Bodet each successive presidential regime, called sexenio for the number of years a president was in power, created and populated new institutions designed to achieve its ends. These institutions tended to remain long after their original purpose was subverted by the policies of a new regime. But what is important from our point of view was the advent of an increasing list of government and government-sponsored institutions that were filled through a system that guaranteed positions for the principal educational stakeholders and political groups within the party.

Accordingly, Jamie Torres Bodet, the architect of the modern system of education worked within the ideological parameters of the system. By the middle 1940s Jamie Torres Bodet signalled the end of the socialist education programme, regarded as chaotic and damaging to the social fabric, and proposed the Escuela de la Unidad Nacional (The School of National Unity). This was the beginning of the idea of educational modernization built around the idea of extending provision to the entire country and expanding higher education to meet the demands of the growing professional middle class dependent on the state and its institutions. Order was to be provided through the issuing of a series of national plans. The first of these was Torres Bodet's *National Plan for the Expansion and Improvement of Primary Teaching (El Plan Nacional para la Expansion y Mejoramiento de la Enseñanza Primaria)*, known popularly as the *Eleven Year Plan (El Plan de Once Años)*, that emphasized a great increase in the quantity and supposedly quality of teachers to be trained, the construction of many more schools and the introduction of a shift system into the majority of schools. However, through agreements with the increasingly powerful teachers' organizations, that later coalesced into the SNTE, the number of hours for teaching was actually reduced.

What Hector Zermeno and Javier Torres Medina (2005, 37) called 'the utopia of expectations' would continue only if certain conditions could be fulfilled. These were as follows: that the motor of industrialization was expanded, as it was in a sometimes peripatetic way until well into the 1970s; that the minimal welfare state, a vital component of corporativist behaviour that operated through state provision and party networking, could continue to function; that the demand for education by the lower social orders did not extend to higher education; that there was not a relative overproduction of professionals; that the logic of economic development did not require at a minimum a relative independence of institutions and of thought; and that the organizations which supposedly represented the interests of educators would remain within the boundaries of the system. That is, the system itself was based on a fragile series of compromises and checks and balances that contained the potential seeds of its own destruction.

The massification of education at all levels led to greater competition for positions that thoroughly alarmed those in charge of maintaining the social order. Gradually the middle class began a process of withdrawing their children from the state sector, through firstly, the setting up of a very large number of primary and secondary schools, secondary schools as appendages of universities, and secondly, sending them to the newly established private universities. Their effective abandonment of the system was to have important consequences.

The Ministry of Education became the one real battleground where compromise between the sectors of the party was difficult to achieve and maintain. If the role of education was to provide the independent and creative thinking necessary for economic development, the ideological and resulting administrative impediments would have to be abandoned. That was unthinkable and created one level of tension between innovators and more consensually oriented administrators who effectively blocked research and new programmes. The administration of the ministry itself and of its satellite organizations was effectively shared with the corporativist organization(s) representing the teachers. In effect, the teachers' organizations had an effective veto over any actions. The teachers' trade union was often divided and this led to a stalemate. The result was largely inconsequential programmes, the inability to translate programmes into action, the suppression of reports, the disappearance of inconvenient sections of the ministry and the evolution of an administration which was top heavy and whose role was one of the negation of initiative and change. Indeed, educational problems were quickly translated into administrative problems and there they remained.

Moreover, there were subtle changes within the middle class itself as a result of these contradictory processes. The professional middle class realized that the historical compromise that led to the corporativist state was blocking its own professional development. In order to keep the peace, they sacrificed their control over their own certification and accepted that the professions were to be regulated through and by the state. Yet they became aware of economic possibilities that could only come to fruition if they were further liberated from the state. As early as 1940 Manuel Gómez Morín (the founder of the conservative Partido de Acción Nacional (PAN)) was disturbed by these blockages. Only when the middle class took fright because of the competition from the marginal social classes in the light of the apparent post-war commitment to human capital theory did they begin to think what until then had been the unthinkable. What aided them in the process was that although they were at least in part financially dependent on the state, much of their lives were now beginning to revolve around the private sector and, more importantly, private education.

The hegemony under pressure (1968–90)

During this period, in order to compensate for the failure to anticipate demand for secondary school places, the government, aware of the possibilities of distance learning based upon the use of television, founded the first *escuelas telesecundarias* (TV secondary schools). Televised broadcasts were used as a backup by learning centres to allow students to have access to teachers. By 1992 broadcasts reached over 9,000 schools. At the same time, aware of the need to control and assess the growing system, the first attempts at evaluation were undertaken. The government through the Secretary of Education, Agustín Yáñez Delgadillo (1958–64), an author and diplomat, also undertook a massive but not entirely successful literacy campaign. However, these actions were overshadowed by a systems crisis resulting from a perceived disjuncture between supply and demand of appropriate positions for the growing professional middle class and their progeny.

By the late 1960s, given the high birth and survival rates, the system of basic and secondary education was oversubscribed. The system of higher education could not cope with what seemed to be the unrealistic demands of students from *nomenklatura* backgrounds to benefit from the same life chances as their families. They shared their aspirations with a new generation of aspiring students in many cases from provincial families. Minor complaints swiftly escalated into the regime's first post-1930's political crisis because of the perception that the system could not absorb all of these students. Another factor was the sheer rigidity of the allocation system and what students, increasingly aware of higher education in other countries, felt was an antiquated curriculum and backward teaching methods. However, despite a series of strikes, unheralded political actions directly attacking the government and a massacre that caught the world's attention just as Mexico was about to host the Olympic Games, the party-state tottered but held firm because the other pillars of the system did not waver. At first the party and the state found it difficult to control the effervescence of a totally middle-class movement based on the fear that their expectations could not be realized; but once order was restored quickly, resorted to a process of co-option.

After the initial round of oppression when scores of people were killed and imprisoned, the new president, Luis Echeverría Álvarez, who as Minister of the Interior had been responsible for the oppression, expanded and liberalized the system of upper secondary and higher education through the skilful creation of state universities up and down the country, as well as establishing specialist institutions to absorb these greater numbers. Important institutions like the Colegio de Ciencias y Humanidades (CCHs), feeder schools for the overstretched National University (UNAM), that served as a model for similar institutions set up by provincial universities – the Colegio de Bachilleres, the Escuelas Nacionales de Estudios Profesionales de la Universidad Nacional Autónoma de México (UNAM) – were established. To solve the numbers crisis and to create a more radical school of higher education with the aim of bringing higher education to the people and absorbing progressive pedagogues like the eminent biologist, Luis Felipe Bojalil Jaber, the Universidad Autónoma Metropolitana (UAM) was established with its three constituent campuses located in poorer parts of Mexico City. Many provincial universities were set up as well as state *institutos tecnológicos*. For those who were nervous about the new massification of education, private universities were established.

These actions, part of what was called the period of reconciliation, set the tone for the years up to 1992. Behind it was the new Minister of Education, the engineer, educationalist and later Oaxacan politician, Dr Victor Bravo Ahúja. He engineered a shift in policy to ensure greater educational coverage for all ages and ushered in an era during which a number of institutions were established whose reach was such that observation and supervision could be widened through the structure and daily activities of these institutions. The Consejo Nacional de Fomento Educativo (CONAFE) was created in 1971 with the aim of providing basic education for those sectors of the population that had not attended a school and to professionalize community leaders. CONAFE took over and centralized many local projects, some of which had been critical of the government.

The advent of CONAFE was accompanied by a complete reconfiguration of the primary school curriculum for which new textbooks were commissioned in order to satisfy some of the demands of local teacher organizations and to circumvent their opposition. Similarly, from 1981 the new Instituto Nacional de Educación de Adultos (INEA) absorbed many local initiatives and applied a centrally determined curriculum using a range of new pedagogic techniques. The system of higher education was expanded and a national grant-giving body CONACyT (the Consejo Nacional de Ciencia y Tecnología) was set up to finance higher degrees and research. The 1973 Education Law was, in part, a synthesis of these innovations and activities that, whilst providing an expanded educational offering and creating thousands of posts in higher education, could only go some way to allaying the fears of the *nomenklatura*, as well as providing centralized control over these organizations.

Successive ministers extended and refined the new, more pervasive and job-creating activities initiated by Bravo Ahúja. In his short time as minister (1976–7) the very charismatic Porfirio Alejandro Muñoz Ledo y Lazo de la Vega produced an encyclopaedic seven-volume set of proposals. His successors, despite the severe economic crisis of the early 1980s, instituted programmes to extend and improve the training of teachers, developed programmes for marginal communities, introduced technology into the curriculum and provided sporting activities in the schools.

Muñoz Ledo's successor, Fernando Solana Morales (1977–82), rationalized Muñoz Ledo's propositions through the Programas y Metas del Sector Educativo (1979–82), which consisted of 52 programmes of which 11 were defined as priorities. In order to catalyse and standardize teacher training with the strong support of the teachers' trade unions he established universities dedicated to the teaching profession, the Universidad Pedagógica Nacional (UPN), and the first of many organizations to provide upper secondary education, Colegio Nacional de Educación Profesional Técnica (CONALEP). In the haste to compensate for what many claimed were years of neglect and inaction, many similar organizations were able to set up their own systems, to such an extent that within a few years there could be up to a dozen competing and sometimes overlapping systems within even a small state. Each had their own agenda and territorial wars were not uncommon.

With the advent of the economic crisis in 1982 there was a pause in the frenetic activity to create all-encompassing institutions. Under Jesús Reyes Heroles, minister from 1982 until his death in 1985, the emphasis was on the rationalization of resources and educational quality. New and overlapping institutions were set up to achieve such a rationalization. Education research was also decentralized to the states themselves; however, they lacked the resources to undertake projects. These efforts were boldly called 'the education revolution' and were spelled out in the Programa Nacional de Educación, Cultura, Recreación y Deporte (1985–8) that elaborated on the need to pay attention to the quality of education through what it called 'the integral formation' of teachers, to give priority to the most deprived areas and to link education to economic development, regional basic education and teacher training. Moreover, by 1982 it appeared that all eligible children could be registered for the first year of primary education. However, this was only possible because non-conventional educational sites were used and a system of community instructors was organized.

The unravelling of the hegemony (1990–)

Converted to the principles of international capital flows, neoliberal policies and the liberation of suppressed talent, the post-1988 governments' impatience with what they regarded as the failed model of state-governed and generated capitalism, experimented with a model that, in theory, opened Mexico to the 'revivifying winds' of internationalism. Hence, Mexico became part of the North American Free Trade Agreement (NAFTA – but called a treaty by the Mexican authorities) and became a member of the Organisation for Economic Co-operation and Development (OECD). The problem was that the model was managed by the same system of institutions that had previously stifled such developments. A tension was created that not only could not easily be resolved but also led to the long-dominant political party actually losing power 12 years later. As we will see, the change, even more brutal than that which occurred during the post-1968 repressive phase, strengthened the underlying structures of control.

The education component of this process of internationalization was initially provided by the post-1994 president, Ernesto Zedillo Ponce de Léon, who as Minister of Education encouraged the stakeholders to sign the Acuerdo Nacional para la Modernización de la Educación Básica y Normal. The novelty of the agreement was that it was intended to officially involve the Mexican business community that would impose its business techniques on the antiquated system of education. The federal government transferred day-to-day control of basic education and teacher training to the states, thereby not only creating another tier of government but also providing employment for professionals. The 31 governors, excluding the federal district, were signatories as well as the SNTE.

The Programa de Modernización de la Educación (1989–94) represented an attempt to apply this latest version of modernization by, yet again, instituting new policies for basic education, teacher training, adult and vocation education, the reorganization of upper secondary education, higher education and postgraduate studies, as well as open systems of education and the introduction of a system of evaluation. Attendance at secondary schools now became obligatory and Article 3 of the constitution was again amended to minimize the social aspects of education. But little could be done to resolve the ongoing problems of inequality, disorganization, inequity and the defects of the system.

Zedillo's government adhered to the same policies but at the same time set up the Programa de Apoyo al Rezago Escolar financed by the World Bank with the intention of directing extra resources to the poorest four states of the country. The 1993 Ley General de Educación and the 1995 Programa de Desarrollo Educativo confirmed these moves and laid the basis for the costs of education to be shared between the federal government, local and state authorities and, in some cases, local organizations of stakeholders.

Neither the much-needed curricular reform of secondary education nor the related need to organize it into a single coherent system was achieved. The 1994 economic crisis put paid to investment in the field of education and the results of national and international evaluations of basic education were so poor that they were not released. Various important changes did take place, such as another recasting of textbooks for basic education, the assignment of additional resources to help students from poor families, new programmes for reading, writing and arithmetic, and attempts to improve higher education through the Fondo para la Modernización de la Educación Superior (FOMES) and the very important Programa para el Mejoramiento del Profesorado (PROMEP). This was designed to upgrade Mexican universities to the level of those in the metropolitan countries as well as the strengthening of technological universities and short degree courses in those areas.

Whilst public spending for education increased during this time, it was not spent efficiently. That is, too much of the budget went into administration and financing the cost of paying over 100,000 teachers who were freed of their teaching responsibilities in order to undertake further study and/or research or be seconded to institutions that existed only on paper. To put things in perspective and without discussing attendance, dropout rates and the quality of education, by the year 2000 it was estimated that about 5 per cent of children and young people between the ages of 6 and 14 were not attending school. Whilst this was an improvement on previous figures, this amounted to about one million children and young people who were receiving no education at all.

Post-2000 developments

In 2000 the ruling party in power in one guise or another since 1917 ceded control to one of the two opposition groups, the Partido de Acción Nacional, an organization that aimed to represent the aspirations of the entire middle class but was divided between traditionalists and neoliberals. It is probably best to characterize the 12 years the PAN was in political control as one of modest change in a time of institutional continuity. Reforms respected the existing structure and even reinforced it. The state and its institutions remained intact, in part, because PAN militants were rewarded with posts within the system. Promises to move towards a meritocracy were never fulfilled and the system continued, albeit populated by new people.

We will discuss these reforms in depth in the following chapters. But it is important to note that the Programa 2001–6 launched by the PAN fully preserved the educational reforms of the previous PRI-led governments, although it paid lip service to the task of radically transforming traditional management practices. Whilst this was regarded as a euphemism by some for breaking the SNTE's effective veto over much educational reform, for more immediate political reasons the PAN sought an accommodation with that organization rather than fulfilling its promise to bring the organization under its control. The leader of the SNTE worked closely with the new minister, Reyes Tamez, and was often in the company of the new president, Vicente Fox Quesada. The very narrow and disputed victory of Felipe Calderón in 2006 was, in part, secured by the SNTE that was rewarded with unheralded power within the SEP and, above all, within basic education, with the son-in-law of the SNTE leader becoming undersecretary. That crucial decision of accommodation that was to mould educational policy until 2012 was couched in terms of combining the best from the past with the promise of the future. The mechanisms long in place continued to operate and were staffed by supporters of the PAN government, many of whom had quickly changed their allegiance from PRI to PAN, and the structures remained the same, with the effect of not making the task of implementing programmes any easier.

The decentralization agenda, which comprised a belated recognition that the federal government could no longer manage the vastly expanded range of programmes and proliferation of institutions, was never properly implemented. Most state governments had neither the personnel nor an administration that could cope because there was no real research base among teachers or even in the state universities. There was little or no mobility between states and the congregation of researchers in Mexico City. There was not the political will to promote transfers of powers to the states, in part, because the central government continued to insist that it alone controlled educational programmes and also the financial arrangements. Local organizations could not cope and the SNTE feared that in certain individual states dissident trade unions could take power and use those bases to launch a national challenge.

Like previous PRI governments the PAN ministry increased the availability of grants for higher education. More importantly, it initiated a special programme to expand intercultural education through the Coordinación General de Educación Intercultural y Bilingüe (CGEIB). In 2002, they established the Instituto Nacional de Evaluación Educativo that over the years was to evolve into a major institution. The government also spent an inordinate amount of money taken from other basic education programmes on what amounted to the creation of an online encyclopaedia crammed with predigested knowledge called the Enciclomedia. It turned out to be the regime's white elephant every bit as much as the PRI regimes' equally poorly thought out and implemented programmes, such as the MICROSEP, designed to install custom-made computers in every school.

The role of educational institutions

We have so far reviewed the expansion of education caused by a combination of what can only be described as a demographic explosion, the growth of expectations and aspirations encouraged by the government, internal social pressures arising from the articulate new middle class and international organizations and agencies that were slowly coming to play an important role in the development of policies. That is, we have provided a socio-historical contextualization of the development of education institutions. We need to further analyse the work of the institutions in charge of education and the role they play in fulfilling the essence of education: namely, learning, selection and control, and above all, how as agencies of a corporative society they are obstacles to meaningful progress.

As we have seen, these institutions had an important role in the transmission of the existing system of values and its distribution. Both consciously and unconsciously they were designed to be control mechanisms to anticipate dissent, buy it off where possible and punish individuals and organizations that acted outside established norms of behaviour. As we will see, the organization of the curriculum and its pedagogy played a significant role in communicating these messages. Over the years the activities of the Ministry of Education greatly expanded through its monopolistic control over curriculum, pedagogy and eventually evaluation. The control was increased when some responsibilities were transferred to the 32 states. State management of the various institutions ranging from preschool to adult education, which were set up as a result of the educational plans and commitments of succeeding sexenios, allowed them greater scrutiny of institutions that previously had at least partly escaped their examination. Internally, the ministry has evolved into three main components: basic education (including such disparate areas as primary education, secondary education, aspects of adult education and many institutions and bodies that were established by successive sexenios), secondary education and higher education. Much later upper secondary education became a separate entity.

The first problem is that activities and tasks were not necessarily divided efficiently according to functions. For example, in the case of upper secondary education as it greatly expanded due to demand, new organizations were created to encourage different aspects of that level, ranging from the academic to various kinds of vocational education and programmes for agriculture and fisheries. It reached the point that by 2000 there were as many as 15 different organizations, each with their own system of upper secondary education. The mix was further complicated because many universities developed their own systems of upper secondary education that in some cases became larger than the university itself and came to dominate it. Each had its own organization, aims, procedures and curriculum. Each organization functioned independently and any efforts to combine them or to develop a generic curriculum were met with institutional opposition, backed up by strong trade-union antagonism and resistance. That is, the very structures designed to promote the various strands of upper secondary education made it impossible for a coherent and rational system to be developed.

The second problem that requires attention is the internal organization of the ministry itself. If we take the case of basic education, by far its largest component, we find that the undersecretary of state for basic education is responsible for a myriad of institutions, some of which maintain a quasi-independent existence, and in some cases, are unknown to the minister and his or her staff. As administrative control was gradually decentralized to the states this created another level that required attention, because not only were the individual 32 state ministries not responsible for their own budgets, unless occasionally supplemented by the state government, they also had little or no input into curriculum design, standards and evaluation. They had special needs and at times required special modifications of a federal initiative, thus involving the federal ministry in further and sometimes difficult tasks. They could also delay a particular programme or project and derail it. Moreover, their internal organization was at times incoherent. They each had specialists in areas like curriculum, pedagogy and the transition from primary to secondary schools but their activities could be countermanded by those responsible for each of the grades. Those responsible tended to come from trade union or civil organizations; they had little real training and often little understanding of what was required to build and maintain a viable and sustainable curriculum. Conflicts arose which could not always be settled by the overburdened federal ministry, and these often boiled over into political conflicts that involved the SNTE and other organizations. That is, the very complex relationship between the federal ministry and the individual states was dysfunctional. The choice of state ministers was governed by the complex system of rewards to the groups making up the state government's ruling parties, and ministers were, in many cases, ill-prepared to deal with education itself. Their job was to accrue power by sometimes seeking the favour of the federal administration and at other times even inventing agencies that were to be the recipient of government funds, which could then be distributed, as we will see, to their personal projects.

Presiding over the increasingly complicated system is the federal ministry. This leads us to examine certain organizational aspects of the federal ministry itself. One such aspect is that many of the new programmes developed by previous sexenios were left in place, and then overlaid by new programmes. In many cases there was considerable overlap between the established and the new institutions, to such an extent that conflicts and incoherences were the order of the day. What complicated matters still further was that in many cases a new minister and his or her sub-secretaries were not always members of the same group and they had to fill the posts at their disposal with nominees of groups who did not support their programmes and often opposed them. Each undersecretaryship was divided into divisions (direcciones) and they were more often than not in conflict when it came to introducing new initiatives. For example, at one point Educación Básica (SEB) was divided into five sections: materials, textbooks, production of books and so on; indigenous education; management and innovation; in-service training; and curriculum development.

The problem is that the overlap between these sections can, in many cases, be so great that in the case of a new initiative, such as the creation of curriculum standards or a generic curriculum, each feels that they have to play the most important part. In this case, in contrast to other divisions, professionals and subject specialists generally staffed the Curriculum Development Division, without allegiance to any of the stakeholders' groups. But these experts could not act as they saw it professionally because some of the other divisions were populated by political nominees who had no real training that was relevant to the generation of a curriculum and were pursuing their own political agendas. The people who filled these positions were beholden to the organization that had nominated them and they could lose their positions with immediate effect if they strayed from the positions put forward and defended by their group. Territorial wars were inevitable and the problem was usually resolved politically and not professionally. Given this, not only would an innovative sub-secretary have to deal with the 32 states but also with sharp divisions within the ministry, and spend an inordinate amount of time trying to negotiate with the various stakeholder groups behind the divisions.

Under these conditions there was no real way forward and in sheer frustration projects were often dropped or so denatured that the end product was of little use in solving the problem it had been set up to solve.

However, what did function was a very intricate system of surveillance within the ministry and between the ministry and the states that allowed the stakeholder organizations to maintain internal and external order, in addition to seeing off any threats to their existence. Their nominees played a key role in this intricate system of checks and balances because their very existence depended upon it.

Looking at the situation of the employees themselves we find that there were in general four types of employee contracts in the SEP. The first corresponded to the legal definition of employee rights and obligations and was the smallest group generally performing the least important tasks and very occasionally the professionals who we discussed earlier. These were what were called the *empleados de base*. Their positions were also underwritten by the SNTE, which meant that aside from extraordinary situations they were immoveable, and to such an extent that, if an employee retired, the post could be passed to a member of the family or in some cases sold to a bidder approved by the trade union. These employees could absent themselves from the post for years at a time, knowing they could come back to it generally at a time of their choosing. In the interim, the post-holder was on a short-term contract (*plaza prestado* or *interino*), which meant that, during their time at the ministry, they enjoyed the same rights as the holder of the post. Many of these holders took much better paid positions abroad but would often return to take up the post, sometimes at short notice, when retirement approached.

Two other types of employees usually filled the higher levels of the ministry, with the exception of highly specialized areas. The first of these was the *empleados de confianza*; these were the teams brought in by the new minister, undersecretaries and area directors. They held their posts only so long as their superiors remained and could also be required to vacate their positions if they lost the confidence of their superiors or if those superiors wished to employ another person. If they failed to conform they would lose their job. Finally, there was another group who occupied *plazas de contrato*. These tended to be highly specialized members of staff in areas like graphic design and computer science, who alone among the employees were sometimes chosen for their expertise and not their political loyalty.

The job insecurity inherent in the system made for a very orthodox approach to projects and a marked reluctance to take decisions without long consultations with their superiors. The superiors themselves could be considered as *de confianza*, because they too were subject to the demands of their own sponsoring organization, the staff of the ministry and outside bodies who saw themselves as potentially affected by any decisions being made. Despite the fact that the teams were loyal to their *caciques*, problems often arose. The situation did not encourage cooperation but it did encourage a system of individual and group surveillance. In the twenty-first century, many were supposedly given greater job security; however, if the definition of their position changed or if they moved to a higher position they lost their legal protection. In other words, the internal organization of the ministry mirrored the hierarchical characteristics of a corporative society. Loyalty to group was paramount and more important than trying to find solutions to education problems.

This meant that in many cases proposals could not be translated into action by group procedures. The problem could in some cases only be solved by charismatic individuals, modern-day 'caudillos', who were the leaders of one of the sponsoring groups, and only after considerable bargaining. This distortion of the system created difficulties with its operations, and underlines the fact that in many cases it could only operate through, what outsiders saw as, corrupt practices.

The educational crisis in perspective

As we have seen, the political system has exhibited increased instability, particularly over the last 20 years, as external factors outside the control of such a national corporativist system began to intrude on Mexico's gradual incorporation into world trading systems and participation in the international social division of labour. Both the material and symbolic grounds were now present for the professional and administrative middle class to consider that its interests could be best served by deserting the system. This in itself was further undermined by the inability of the corporativist state to provide a safety net for its traditional supporters, in the context of a series of severe economic crises that began at the end of the 1970s.

One of the battlegrounds was education, not only for the reasons we have identified above but also because of its absolutely vital role within a corporativist state and for its administrators and apologists, that is, the non-entrepreneurial middle class. The non-entrepreneurial middle class itself was pulled in several different directions. Whilst its role in the state was one that offered prestige and, above all, protection, it was aware of its shortcomings and the literature is replete with calls for the independence of the professions and the need for economic freedom from the state. Again, this middle class increasingly felt under threat with the expansion of higher education and the fear that hitherto marginal social groups could compete successfully with it for jobs.

Those who could do so educated their children privately but it was not an altogether happy situation because private education was vitiated with the same system of networking which hallmarked the more general socio-political system. The education this growing sector imparted was not superior to that offered by the state sector and the majority of these institutions were unprincipled establishments for the awarding of degrees and often unable to undertake basic research nor offer subjects which required a large capital investment. Competition resulting from international protocols like the Free Trade Agreement negotiated with the United States and Canada, rather than opening up opportunities, seemed in the eyes of the middle class to lead to an emigration of the better-awarded posts to those countries, leaving only middle management positions available within Mexico itself.

Hence, the very success of creating a larger and for the first time relatively independent educational elite also included its own seeds of destruction. The system began to produce too many potential members to be absorbed into the bureaucracy. Many found positions in expanding universities and later non-governmental organizations initially established to attempt to control marginal social groups. By the early 1990s the consensus that led to an education system dedicated to social control at the cost of economic development was clearly unravelling. For the first time, a coherent and direct attack was made upon this consensus. In a telling series of essays reminiscent of Fabian tracts, educationalists prompted by Gilberto Guevara Niebla (1981, 1992) wrote of the 'silent scandal' hidden for so long by the authorities from the public in the name of an incoherent ideology. Every indicator, he and others argued, showed that since 1946 educational institutions and practices had failed to deliver at all levels. Mexico could neither fulfil the aspirations of its population nor compete in the international social division of labour except through providing the menial labour required by the *maquiladora* (assembly line) industries established in the US-bordering states. But the public they addressed did not heed their words. The non-entrepreneurial middle class, their potential audience, was totally integrated into the system of networking and was not in a position to find its own voice. Yet for the first time the work of those marginalized by the system in the past, like Carlos Muñoz, Pablo Latapí, Maria de Ibarrola, Carlos Ornelas, Jean-Pierre Vielle and Sylvia Schmelkes, to name a very few, become crucial. It is not our intention to suggest that there were no critiques of government policy prior to this time. The point is that these critiques were marginalized owing to the transient importance given to educational research and, more importantly, the lack of an audience. The growth of further and higher education, the expansion of the middle class and the founding of journals began to change this. Our point here is only to indicate that these critiques did not have much influence until the 1980s.

One element that guaranteed the relative independence of the middle class in Europe, its periodic alliances with working-class movements, continued to be absent in Mexico. And this was crucial in terms of the establishment of educational institutions and practices. In Mexico, the middle class was a creation of the state and functioned as a dependency of it. Because there was no large independent middle class, as there was in some Latin American countries, its hegemony in education was replaced by hierarchies and a rigid paternalism. Above all, during a transitional period we find the substitution of an educational elite which had perfected its mechanisms for one which did not have these skills in the modalities of social control.

Without those alliances, the middle class could never mould institutions in its image and according to its expectations. The possibilities of an alliance – as found in France, Germany and Britain – with these social groups and educational professionals was difficult if not impossible to achieve. This was to lead to another crisis in Mexico: the relative alienation of the teaching profession from the middle class and its retreat into a protective immobilism, an issue that we address in the last chapter. In the next chapter we examine curriculum, pedagogic and assessment reforms in the Mexican education system.

3
Curriculum, Pedagogic and Assessment Reforms in the Mexican System

In Mexico, the history of the curriculum runs in parallel with the history of curriculum studies, with the two barely meeting at any point. In the first instance, we need to understand the possibilities of and problems with the different versions of the curriculum as they were originally conceived. That is, we need to understand what these curriculum notions are, what disciplinary limits they have and how they connect to other fields of study. The concept of curriculum is characterized by its polysemic and contested nature. The most common thread running through the history of both the enacted curriculum and the theory of curriculum in Mexico, though these should never be treated as equivalents, is that of its practicality, examples of which are intervention plans, study plans and programmes. Alfredo Furlan (2011) described this separation between theorization and practices as between the curriculum 'as thought' and the curriculum 'as lived'. He also suggested that the focus on study plans has meant that work on structures, values and models, and providing a justification for these, had been neglected. In general, curriculum problems were defined in practical terms, so that issues that were addressed included: overcrowding and the quality of teaching; alleged deficiencies in academic, communicative and scientific competencies among primary and secondary school students; and the absence of connections between what is learnt in schools and life experiences. However, some attention was paid to understanding the curriculum in relation to those social, political and educational processes that inform it. For example, the Mexican Council for Educational Research (COMIE) commissioned in the 1980s and the 1990s two evaluations of curriculum research (see also Diaz Barriga et al., 1995, and Diaz Barriga, 2003), and these sought to address fundamental curriculum questions.

Frida Diaz Barriga (2007) identified four important curriculum tendencies at both the theoretical and practice levels, though she also noted the difficulties of operating through these theoretical frameworks in Mexican classrooms: i) the systemic-technological; ii) the critical-reconceptualist; iii) the psycho-pedagogical or cognitive constructionist approach; and iv) the interpretive. To these should be added neoliberal curriculum frameworks, focusing on competences and extra-national single-surface comparative and assessment-driven implementation mechanisms.

The systemic-technological curriculum

Mexican curriculum research during the 1970s focused on interventions, and in particular, the design of study plans and programmes underpinned by frameworks of technological rationality and behaviourist psychology. These works were structured round Ralph Tyler's (1950, 1968) four evaluative questions: What educational objectives should be reached? Which educative experiences allow us to reach them? How can these experiences be efficiently organized? How should we evaluate the achievement of these objectives? In Mexico, the design of study programmes by objectives and through the use of what was held as the scientific method were formulated by Glazman and de Ibarrola (1976), The Commission for New Teaching Methods (1976), Huerta (1981) and Gago (1982). All of these influential Mexican academics and members of the commission proposed frameworks through which the actual Mexican curriculum could be structured; though as we have seen in Chapter 2, intentions are rarely the same as actual practices.

This movement and its technical-rationality underpinnings emanated from the curriculum movement in the United States that can be traced back to the beginning of the twentieth century. Two key figures are representative of this surge of enthusiasm for the application of the scientific method to the study and implementation of the curriculum. John Franklin Bobbitt and Werrett Charters in their different ways argued for precision, objectivity, prediction and the use of the scientific method to establish once and for all what should be taught in schools, and, indeed, how educational knowledge should be structured. Bobbitt's two major works were, appropriately enough, *The Curriculum* (1918) and *How to Make a Curriculum* (1924), and in 1913, he published a long article entitled, 'Some General Principles of Management Applied to the Problems of City-school Systems' (1913). Charters' two major works were *Methods of Teaching: Developed from a Functional Standpoint* (1909) and *Curriculum Construction* (1923), both of which reflected then currently fashionable ideas of structural functionalism.

Bobbitt's work provides an early example of the arguments for behavioural objectives and he is credited with developing a notion of objective analysis whereby designated skills are broken down into their constituent elements. These skills were derived from the activities of experts in a variety of fields essential to the well-being of society. Bobbitt claimed that curricular aims and objectives could be derived from an objective examination of these activities. Furthermore, these skills and their component sub-skills could be expressed as specific teaching objectives, which are so arranged that the curriculum is designed around them. His work was behaviourist in that he understood learning as the acquiring of these skills and the evaluation of sets of behaviours, so as to determine whether the learner had successfully acquired these skills. It is easy to see here the origin of the behavioural objectives movement which influenced curriculum making in the 1970s and 1980s in Mexico and which continues to shape global, national and local curricula round the world.

What is noteworthy is the underpinning belief in science as the model for the essential practical activity of determining what should be included in a curriculum and how it should be delivered. Atomism, pre-specification and control are therefore foregrounded, with the curriculum conceptualized in terms of behavioural objectives and an input–output model of schooling. Ralph Tyler (1950, 1968), for example, advocated a means-end approach to the development of the curriculum. He believed that educational aims could only be articulated in terms of objectives and that these preceded learning experiences and the evaluation of what is learnt. Curriculum making was understood as a linear process which starts with the development of clear objectives or goals, proceeds through to the selection of content that is specified in behavioural terms – its acquisition must be an observable or testable process – and finishes with the evaluation of that process to see if those objectives have been met. However, he did not believe that objectives could be specified in precise behavioural terms, and he believed that they should be kept at a fairly general level. His work has influenced current models of curriculum development, though his objectives approach has in turn been criticized for its limited understanding of the enacted curriculum. Other theorists such as W. H. Popham (1972) were less discriminating about the use of behavioural objectives and were enthusiastic advocates of a scientific view of curriculum making. Such a position was underpinned by an empiricist view of knowledge that coloured their perception of the curriculum.

Behaviourism is a philosophical theory and has been used specifically within the discipline of education to provide an explanation for the play of social and educational objects in history. It makes three interrelated claims. The first is that if investigators are trying to understand a human being's psychology, they should not be concerned with what is in the person's mind but with how that person behaves. The second claim is that behaviours can be fully and comprehensively explained without recourse to any form of mental construct or event. The source of these behaviours is the environment and not the mind of the individual. And the third claim which behaviourists are likely to make and which follows from the first two claims is that if mental terms are used as descriptors, then they should be replaced by behavioural terms or, at least, those mental constructs should be translated into behavioural descriptors.

Behaviourism as a theory of learning then suffers from a number of misconceptions. Because of its strictures against immaterial mental substances – agents endowed with the capacity to operate outside embodied, socially derived or genetic causal impulses – and the internal conversation in learning (see Archer, 2007), behaviourism is now rarely thought of as a coherent or convincing theory of learning. A number of problems with it have been identified, particularly the claim that a theory of human learning is not sufficient unless reference is made to non-behavioural mental states – cognitive, representational or interpretive. In particular, this refers to the way an individual represents the world in relation to how they have done so in the past, and how this is conditioned by institutional, systemic, embodied and discursive structures; stories, narratives, arguments and chronologies, and structures of agency. A second reason for rejecting behaviourism is the existence of internal or inner processing activities. We feel, intuit, experience and are aware of our own inner mental states in the learning process. To reduce these phenomenal qualities to behaviours or dispositions to behave is to ignore the immediacy and instantaneous nature of those processes which condition learning. Finally, it is suggested that reducing learning to individual reinforcement histories is to develop an impoverished or incomplete theory, and consequently marginalize pre-existing structures, developed schemata, complex inner lives, prior representations and structural enablements and constraints, which allow learning to take place.

Critical-reconceptualist curriculum approaches

This behavioural objectives movement in Mexico was challenged in the late twentieth century by more critical approaches to the study of the curriculum and therefore implicitly by radical instrumentalist views of what should constitute a curriculum and how it should be constructed. Mexican scholars made important contributions to this critical-reconceptualist view, and in curriculum terms, focused on issues such as the cultural and ideological hegemony of imperialist influences, in the case of Mexico predominantly Spanish and United States ones, and critical pedagogic frameworks. Mexican scholars who worked to this framework at this time included Angel Díaz Barriga, Alfredo Furlan, Eduardo Remedi, Margarita Panza and others. An example of a curricular project in this vein was the development of a modular system at the Metropolitan Autonomous University of Xochimilco. This project deliberately set its face against a knowledge curriculum based round the academic disciplines. It developed a multidisciplinary and integrative version of academic knowledge, and identified a set of important social problems for each of the professions, which became known as the objectives of transformation, or *objetos de transformación*.

Critical pedagogy is instrumentalist in design and is underpinned by a belief that schooling and the curriculum always represents a preparation for, and legitimation of, a particular form of life (see also McLaren, 1989). Through pedagogic means, it therefore seeks to surface, and in the process, disrupt, conventional forms of understanding which serve to reproduce undemocratic, racist, sexist and unequal social relations. The task of critical pedagogy is to unmask hegemonies and critique ideologies with the political and ethical purpose of helping to empower students and more generally, the social groups to which they belong (see also Lankshear et al., 1996). Unlike some postmodern viewpoints, critical pedagogy is predicated on a clear ethical position with regards to society and to the way society reproduces itself, though some versions of critical pedagogy emphasize the need to disrupt conventional school knowledge structures and the reproductive processes that accompany them, without specifying alternative frames of reference for students. The end point becomes the disruptive process rather than the reforming of schooling and society in a particular way.

Critical pedagogy has had to wrestle with a number of serious problems. Though implicit within it is a notion of student-centredness and student empowerment, all too frequently Mexican teachers found it difficult to forgo their role as orchestrators of proceedings, thus in effect critical pedagogy became a means by which one ideological viewpoint replaced another. Structural constraints on the implementation of critical pedagogic processes proved to be strong impediments to delivery in Mexico, and indeed, the state sought to reinforce the power of those structural constraints with the result that alternative pedagogies proved difficult to enact. An example in Mexico was the way the state imposed a national curriculum and appropriate methods for teaching it by strengthening evaluation and assessment arrangements, through such devices as the Evaluación Nacional del Logro Académico en Centros Escolares (ENLACE). Students also found it difficult to give voice to their own localized and immediately available experiential knowledge within the constraints of a formal curriculum and a formal process of schooling. The concentration on class, gender and race led to an essentialized, reductionist and as a consequence, oversimplified view of identity formation; and the political ideals that underpinned critical pedagogy were frequently abstracted and decontextualized so that the movement itself lost impetus. Finally, critical pedagogy never developed beyond a system of ideas so that the relationship between culture and practice was never adequately operationalized.

To these problems and issues should be added the inability of critical pedagogy to confront the postmodern attack on foundationalism, both epistemological and more importantly ethical. In turn, critical pedagogy lost ground to technicist frameworks of understanding, which allowed governments in Mexico and round the world to set in place organizational and pedagogic structures antithetical to critical pedagogy.

Psycho-pedagogical or cognitive constructionist approaches

A third curricular movement, identified by Frida Diaz Barriga, was what she describes as psycho-pedagogical approaches to the curriculum. This movement emphasized new forms of knowledge organization and innovative teaching approaches. Its origins and hence underpinnings related to constructivist and constructionist pedagogies associated with scholars from all over the world, such as David Ausubel, Jerome Bruner, Joseph Novak, César Coll, Philippe Perrenoud and Lev Vygotsky. Beginning in the 1970s and extending far beyond this were a series of research projects focusing on the curriculum, its sociocultural formation and its amalgamation of curriculum studies with teaching didactics.

There is a range of theories that might be labelled as constructivist. For example, Jerome Bruner (1996) distinguishes between symbol-processing views of learning, which he rejects, and sociocultural or constructivist views of learning. Typically, he avoids taking up a position in which these two theories of learning are seen as polar opposites, so that if one position is advocated, any reference to the other is excluded. However, he does want to draw clear lines and boundaries between them. The first of these theories, the computational or symbol-processing view, conceptualizes learning as a threefold process of sorting, storing and retrieving coded information which has been received from an external source, and this mirrors the way a computer processes data. The mind is a *tabula rasa*, and learning comes from experience and perception. Information or data is inputted into the mind, and this consists of predigested facts, which represent in a clear and unambiguous way how the world works. The theory of mind that this represents conceptualizes each act of learning in input and output terms, and this assimilative process means that, as a result of the learning process, adjustments are made to the store of facts and theories that the person already holds, in the light of new information that the learner receives. This is a mechanistic process, and the notion of interpretation is subsequently reduced to the assimilation of new information and the reformulation of the mindset of the learner. Learning is understood as a passive reflection of the world, with particular learning episodes being understood as more or less efficiently realized.

Symbol-processing approaches have their origins in the philosophical theory of empiricism, proponents of which understand the world as given and then received by individual minds. This theoretical framework separates out language from reality, mind from body and the individual from society (see also Bredo, 1999). The first of these, the language-reality split, suggests that facts can be collected about the world, which are atheoretic and separate from the belief systems of the collector. These facts are understood as true statements about the world. Furthermore, the theory of learning which emanates from this points to the need to discover what they are, and then develop appropriate models to explain them. The claim being made here is that language is a transparent medium and has the capacity to faithfully represent what is external to it. There is, however, a more appropriate solution to the problem of the relationship between mind and reality and this is that representations of reality are not given in a prior sense because of the nature of reality, or because the mind is constructed in a certain way, but as a result of individual human beings actively constructing and reconstructing that reality in conjunction with other human beings, some contemporary, some long since dead. This brings to the fore the dispute between constructivists and situated cognitivists, in that the former suggest that this active process of learning occurs in the mind, whilst the latter locate the process of categorizing, classifying and framing the world in society and not in individual minds.

Symbol-processing approaches to cognition also suggest a further dualism, between mind and body. This separation of mind and body locates learning and cognition in the mind, as it passively receives from the bodily senses information that it then processes. The mind is conceived of as separate from the material body and from the environment in which the body is located. Learning is understood as a passive process of acquiring information from the environment. Sociocultural theorists take issue with the supposed passivity of the process, and want to build into it active and transformational elements. There is a third dualism that critics of symbol-processing approaches have suggested is problematic. This is the separation of the individual from society. If a learner is given a task to complete, they have to figure out for themselves what the problem is and how it can be solved. The task is framed by a set of social assumptions made by the teacher. The problem with the symbol-processing view is that an assumption is made that the task and the way it can be solved are understood in the same way by both the learner and the teacher. However, this is an assumption which should not be made. One of the consequences of making it is that the learner who then fails to solve the problem is considered to be inadequate in some specified way, rather than someone who has reconfigured or interpreted the problem in a way incongruent with that of the teacher or observer. The individual/civic distinction, which is central to a symbol-processing view of cognition, separates out individual mental operations from the construction of knowledge by communities and this leaves it incomplete as a theory of learning.

A particular iteration of socio-cultural or constructivist theories is cultural-historical activity theory. That there now is a three-generation model of cultural-historical activity theory is part of its formation as an established theory (see also Engeström, 2001). This and each generation of activity theory can be understood in two distinct ways. The first is in terms of its historical trajectory, so it is possible to understand Lev Vygotsky's (1978) theory of mediation as a reaction against what it emerged from. It sought to replace the stimulus-response model of the behaviourists because it became apparent that there were aporias, gaps, contradictions and muddles in the theory itself (the theory in short was inadequate); or it can be understood as an attempt to frame the concept as a universalizing category. Both of these versions have meta-theoretical and thus universalizing elements, insofar as the first requires a theory of history and the second requires a theory of social psychology. However, these universalizing elements are framed in different ways.

The first set of cultural-historical activity theory (CHAT) studies was inspired by Lev Vygotsky, and as its centrepiece, had the well-known triangular model of subject, object and mediating artefact. When people engage in a learning activity (and in a sense, this constitutes the principal activity of consciousness) they do so by interacting with the material world around them (though here the material world is embodied, structured and discursive). What they are doing is entering into a social practice, which is mediated by artefacts. This needs to be qualified in two ways. Firstly, there cannot be an unmediated practice, so, for example, a discursive practice cannot be atheoretic, and secondly, that as a consequence it is not possible to have direct access to the practice itself. Indeed, it is difficult to understand the idea of a practice which is separate from the way it is mediated for us. For Vygotsky, our contacts with people and their environments are mediated by artefacts, such as physical tools, technologies or social norms. This in turn led Vygotsky to a preoccupation with the notion of meaning and thus to the development of a notion of semiotic mediation and in particular to a rejection of the behaviourist paradigm, which posited a passive object-to-subject relationship.

Learning can be seen as adaptive rather than transformative, and Vygotsky's work has always been associated with the latter rather than the former. However, the notions of adaptation and transformation are complex. The idea of adaptation would suggest that what is learnt conforms to those sets of behaviours, norms and strategies which constitute the social world, and which are external to the learner. The learner enters into a state of equilibrium, so that what is inside the mind of the learner (this changes) is now synchronized with what is outside the mind of the learner (which has not undergone any change at all). On the other hand, a transformative approach would suggest that both the mind of the learner and the object in the environment have changed. What this implies is not that one theory is misguided and should be replaced by another – a better account of a practice – but that there is a need to build into the theory being developed the possibility that some learning is adaptive and some is transformatory.

Four issues are of concern here. The first relates to whether meaning resides in the object itself or is created in conjunction with or through the interaction between subject and object. The second relates to the idealist tendencies in Vygotsky's thought (see also Bakhurst, 2009). The third issue is that all these mediating devices are expected to work in the same way, even though they have different grammars and constitutions. And what follows from this, specifically in relation to learning, is that it is hard to believe that every interaction has an equal possibility of influencing and thus changing the learning environment. For Vygotsky, the focus of his analysis was tool mediation and the activity system where these mediations occurred, rather than the individual per se. However, what is being suggested here is that this activity can be transformational both for the system (or learning environment) and for the individual, but not in every circumstance.

Many of the curriculum initiatives in Mexico, underpinned as they were by constructivism, failed at the classroom level. The reasons for this failure are many and varied, and we have identified some of them in Chapter 2. Ashwani Kumar (2011) suggests that the philosophical and operational requirements of implementing a constructivist curriculum fundamentally clash with the administrative and managerial culture of the Mexican education system. In addition, and as we have noted, there are serious conceptual flaws in constructivist understandings of curriculum, pedagogy and learning. This has meant that the Mexican school system was able to embrace pedagogies, learning approaches and assessment practices inspired by behaviourist and technical-rationality thinking, but it was not able to implement constructivist pedagogies because the system has never been able to abandon a centralized, transmissive and authoritarian educational administrative and curriculum approach.

An interpretivist curriculum

The fourth of Díaz Barriga's curriculum tendencies is interpretivism. Those studies that broadly fit into this framework understand the curriculum from a phenomenological or ethnomethodological position; for example, interactionism, hermeneutics and psychoanalysis. All these broadly phenomenological positions, and there are many still being subscribed to in Mexico and round the world, sought to emphasize the role of interpretation and human volition in both understanding the curriculum and in projects of implementation. As with constructivism, implementing curriculum projects underpinned by a notion of interpretivism in Mexico has generally failed to change practice at the level of the classroom.

In contrast to behaviourist perspectives on learning then, there are phenomenological approaches. Phenomenology is a meta-philosophy that focuses on the three key aspects of learning, the relationship of the individual to and with the world involving a process of change, the subsequent conception and activation of being in the world and how our descriptions, words, schema and theories can provide us with some purchase on that world. The focus is on the givens of immediate experience and this is an attempt to capture that experience as it is lived, both by the individual and the external observer. This knowledge-making activity is directed in the first instance to the things in themselves that are the objects of consciousness, and that try to find 'a first opening' (Merleau-Ponty, [1945] 1962) on the world, free of those presuppositions brought to any learning setting. This entails a learning methodology which foregrounds subjective experiences and understands them in their own terms, both linguistically and conceptually, whilst at the same time treating these two modes separately. This presupposes that the experience of others is accessible to us, even if with the greatest of difficulty. And this points to the break with behaviourism that phenomenologists generated. Whereas behaviourists were concerned above all with the behaviour of individuals and eschewed the inner workings of the mind, phenomenologists understood behaviour and consciousness as essential to any theory of learning. They are different aspects of the same phenomena; the world as it is lived by the individual and as it is known by that individual and others.

Neoliberal curricula in Mexico

Governments round the world and coordinators and curriculum developers of systems of education such as the Mexican school system at the end of the twentieth century – with a few notable exceptions – have reached an agreement about the nature of the school curriculum, learning approaches and assessment practices. This consensus now operates at all levels of education systems, and can be expressed in terms of a number of propositions. Traditional forms of knowledge and strong insulations between them need to be preserved; each of these knowledge forms can be expressed in terms of lower-and higher-level domains, and the latter have to be taught before the former and sequenced correctly; knowledge can be constructed in behaviourist terms; certain groups of children are better able to access the curriculum than other children, and, as a result, a differentiated curriculum is necessary to meet the needs of all school learners. The teacher's role is to impart this body of knowledge in the most effective way, and thus their brief cannot concern itself with the ends to which education is directed but only the means for its efficient delivery, and the school's role is to deliver a public service that meets the targets set for it by governments and other such educational systems.

Within this technicist framework, assessment plays a key role. A summative assessment specifies those knowledge sets, skills or dispositions that a learner is required to have, and which are expressed in such a way that they can be tested in a controlled environment, such as an examination. The principal problem with neoliberal assessment procedures of this type is that testing a person's knowledge, skills and dispositions is likely to have washback effects on the original set. Instead of the assessment process acting exclusively as a descriptive device, it also acts in a variety of ways to transform the curriculum it is seeking to measure. Washback effects work on a range of objects and in different ways. So, for example, there are washback effects on the curriculum, on teaching and learning, on the capacity of the individual and more fundamentally, on the structures of knowledge, though these four mechanisms are frequently conflated in the minds of educational stakeholders. Micro washback effects work directly on the person, whereas macro washback effects work directly on institutions and systems, which then subsequently have an impact on individuals within those institutions and systems. Finally, a learner may have to reframe their knowledge or skill set to fit the test, and therefore the assessment of their mastery of this knowledge or skill is not a determination of their competence. Instead it shows whether they have successfully understood how to rework their capacity to fit the demands of the examination technology. As a result, teaching to the test occurs and the curriculum is narrowed to accommodate those learning outcomes that can more easily be assessed. There is some evidence of this having occurred with ENLACE, the now defunct Mexican system of nationwide assessment and evaluation.

Diaz Barriga (2003) identified in 2003 nine underpinning principles characterizing curriculum reforms in Mexico. (We have added to and extended some of them.) Since then, little has changed, though the abolition of ENLACE in 2015 may signify a small movement away from neoliberal policies and practices. The first of these is that a curriculum should be based round a set of competences, though the whole notion of a competency is poorly understood and ill-defined. The second principle is curricular flexibility and the third is an administrative focus on strategic planning and quality control in curriculum development and evaluation. These had important effects on the contents and form of the Mexican basic curriculum. As we have seen, some attempts have been made to base the curriculum round psycho-pedagogical constructivism and cognitive and sociocultural psychology, but this has rarely been applied successfully. In addition, there has been an adherence to curriculum frameworks being developed by international bodies such as the Organisation for Economic Co-operation and Development (OECD). The Mexican curriculum at the basic level has been reformulated to fit with the precepts underlying the curriculum contents and processes espoused by the OECD and its measurement arm, the Programme for International Student Assessment (PISA).

The sixth principle is the adoption of a curriculum which is focused on a theory–practice integration and a notion of professional formation (pre-service) and re-formation (in-service) that is practice-based and situated in real-life settings, such as classrooms, though as we will see in Chapter 4, notions of productive learning environments for these new teachers are misunderstood and inadequately conceptualized. Teaching and curricular programmes centred on problem-solving methodologies, known as problem-based learning, and case analysis have been implemented. However, these generally compete unsuccessfully with instructional and textbook-based forms of didactics. There has also been attempts to incorporate new themes or fields of knowledge in the development of curriculum projects, described as curricular themes or transversal axes, such as sustainable economic development, human rights, values education, civic-mindedness and new technological developments. These however do not sit well in an assessment-driven curriculum. And finally, there have been projects to incorporate information and communication technologies into curriculum and pedagogic practices, though these have been underfunded in some of the Mexican states and particularly with indigenous communities. As we have suggested in this chapter and the previous one, many of these projects and proposals have met strong resistance at the classroom level, besides also constituting regressive and muddled notions of what a curriculum and a curricular practice might be.

The rhetoric of Mexican curriculum reform is marked by a set of constructs, such as innovation, competency, flexibility, quality, excellence, student-centred pedagogy, child-centredness, experiential learning, problem-based learning, information and communication technology and integrated thematic pedagogy. Each of these, in order for them to be understood as they are used in actual practices, needs to be contextualized in relation to technicist standards of certification and evaluation, audit cultures, extra-national systems of assessment and evaluation, and instrumentalist (in particular economistic) forms of curriculum delivery, many of these familiar to people working in the Mexican system. (For example, the 2013 UNESCO Report about the Mexican education system made a series of recommendations that were underpinned by technical-rationalist ways of thinking.) A competency curriculum is an example of this. For some in Mexico, a competency means a skill, for others a disposition and even a transposition of disciplinary knowledge to a future capacity. The argument is that Mexico should be focusing on, as PISA claims to be doing, competent and flexible entrepreneurs ready to solve problems in future settings that may not be currently understood or even envisaged. This is in effect a knowledge-based curriculum where competency-based study plans are reinstated based on behavioural objectives and conformity to a higher authority. However, despite all the talk in Mexican universities and governmental curriculum departments, teachers continue to teach in the same way that they have been doing for years.

The enacted curriculum

A curriculum, in essence, is a planned programme of learning, and therefore if we are to understand it, we also have to develop a theory of learning. As a concept, learning is fundamentally related to knowledge, and therefore if we are thinking about learning and the practices of learning, we also need to make reference to what is to be and how it is learned, and typically what we are aiming at in such considerations is some form of knowledge. Philosophers usually divide knowledge into two principal categories, knowing-that and knowing-how. (They sometimes also add a third category, knowing-by-acquaintance, but this is not central to the argument being made.) The suggestion here is that these forms of knowledge are fundamentally different; in other words, that there are strong and impermeable boundaries between them. We want to suggest that this is misleading, and that consequently, some of the problems that these strong insulations have created can be resolved. This has implications for our theory of learning and knowledge development, and therefore for any curriculum theory that follows from it. What also follows from this is that in society these different forms of knowledge are given different statuses or have different attachments of importance; so, for example, vocational knowledge (broadly thought of as being about processes) is considered to be less important than academic knowledge (broadly understood as being about propositions), but these ascriptions of importance do not lie in the intrinsic nature of each knowledge form but in the way these knowledge forms are realized in particular societies.

Knowledge then, is fundamental to three types of learning that can be identified: cognitive (relating to propositions), skill-based (relating to processes) and dispositional (relating to embodiments). Cognition comprises the manipulation of those symbolic resources (words, numbers, pictures, etc.), which points to (though not necessarily in a mirroring or isomorphic sense) something outside itself, though the referent might also be construed as internally related, or more specifically, as a part of an already established network of concepts (for example, see also Brandom, 2000). Skill-based knowledge is different from cognition because it is procedural and not propositional. Dispositional knowledge refers to relatively stable habits of mind and body, sensitivities to occasion and participation repertoires. Distinguishing between knowledge of how to do something (or process forms of knowledge), knowledge of something (or, in Brandom's terms, judging that claim in terms of its relations within and to a network of concepts) and embodied forms of knowledge (assimilating an action and being able to perform in the spaces associated with that action) is important. However, they are in essence all knowledge-making activities, and furthermore can be formulated generically as acts of learning.

Knowledge is transformed at the pedagogic site, so it is possible to suggest that qualities such as, the simulation of the learning object, the representational mode of the object, its degree and type of amplification, control in the pedagogic relationship, progression or its relations with other learning objects (i.e. curriculum integration), the type of pedagogic text, relations with other people in the learning process, the organization of time (temporal relations) and types of feedback mechanism are fundamental components of this pedagogic transformation. What this means is that in the learning process, the learning object takes a new form as a result of changes to its properties: simulation, representation, amplification, control, integration, textual form, relations with other people, time and feedback.

Theoretical and contextual considerations impact, then, on how elements of teaching and learning are realized. Acknowledging this allows the identification of a number of learning models: assessment for learning, observation, coaching, goal-clarification, mentoring, peer learning, simulation, instruction, concept formation, reflection, metacognitive learning, problem-solving and practice. And each of these in turn is underpinned by a particular theory of learning. What this means is that any model of learning that is employed, is constructed in relation to particular views of how we can know the world and what it is. These models or learning sets (and this includes feedback mechanisms of a particular kind) give different emphases to the various elements of a learning process.

Choosing between these models depends on the nature and constitution of the learning object; in other words, the former is logically dependent on the latter. It also depends on the choice of learning theory that is made. These learning models have a crucial role to play (whichever one is chosen) in processes of learning and constitute elements of Bernstein's (1998) pedagogic device.

Curriculum and assessment practices

The enacted curriculum then is the end point of a process of recontextualization (Bernstein, 1998), from the original construction of knowledge to its reconfigured form at the pedagogic site. However, Bernstein's term is seriously misleading in that it seems to refer to a change in the context rather than a change in the formulation of knowledge (i.e. constructs, skills and dispositions) as it is being used in particular circumstances and contexts. The second important point to consider in trying to plot the formation of the enacted Mexican curriculum over time is that curriculum formations are not uniform and uniformly delivered in any education system. Consequently, we can observe examples (moments and traces) of particular curriculum formations, that is, the systemic-technological, the critical-reconceptualist, the psycho-pedagogical or cognitive constructionist approach, the interpretive and the cluster of curriculum models that can be fitted into a neoliberal perspective, in the history and evolution of the Mexican education system, but rarely in their totality.

We can focus on two pedagogical initiatives in the history of the system: The Comprehensive Reform of Basic Education (Reforma Integral de la Educación Básica (RIEB)) and the introduction and subsequent cancellation of the Evaluación Nacional del Logro Académico en Centros Escolares (ENLACE). The Reforma Integral de la Educación Básica's key elements include the coordination of the different levels of basic education: continuity between pre-primary, primary and lower secondary education, and an emphasis on issues relevant for today's society and education for life. The reform involved the preparation of updated study plans and programmes, focusing on clearly defined expectations of skills to be acquired by grade and subject, improved training for school directors and teachers, and the implementation of participative processes of school management.

The RIEB is based on a number of pedagogical principles: student-centred learning processes; planning in order to stimulate learning; the creation of productive learning environments; collaborative work to develop learning; an emphasis on the development of competences, the achievement of curricular standards and expected learning outcomes (Estándares Curriculares y Aprendizajes Esperados); the use of educational materials to promote learning; assessment for learning; the promotion of inclusion to address diversity; the integration of issues of social relevance; the renewal of the pact between the student, the teacher, the family and the school; a reorientation of leadership practices and expectations; and offering pedagogical support to the schools. However, these concepts are poorly understood and in many cases directly contradict others.

The study plan for basic education (based as it is on the Jesuitical Ratio Studiorum dating from 1599) comprises the following: 12 pedagogical principles; five life competencies to be developed across all stages of basic education; lifelong learning, information management, management of situations, coexistence and life in society; the profile of a basic education graduate, which specifies 10 characteristics (e.g. 'uses the mother tongue, orally and in writing, to communicate clearly and fluently and interact in distinct social and cultural contexts; in addition, has basic tools to communicate' (Government of Mexico, 2004)); the curricular map of basic education, which specifies the four fields of education for basic education (language and communication, mathematical thinking, exploration and understanding of the natural and social world, and personal and social development); as well as the subjects associated with each field of education, their distribution across grades and the time allocated to them in the timetable; curricular references/parameters for indigenous education and the establishment of principles and objectives for the national curriculum to be adapted to indigenous education. It also specifies the purposes of the creation of a subject of indigenous language, strategies for the development of digital competencies (including performance indicators about teachers' use of ICT in their teaching), principles for the management of schooling and learning (including the management of schools' timetables) and the structure for the organization of curricular standards. These express what students are expected to know and be able to do at the end of the four main stages of basic education: pre-primary education, third grade, sixth grade and lower secondary education; for each education field and subject, they have a given structure. For instance, curricular standards for Spanish are grouped into five components: reading processes and interpretations of texts; the production of written texts; the production of oral texts and participation in communication events; knowledge of the characteristics, function and use of language and attitudes in language. A particular national standard for reading ability was also introduced for each grade: the number of words a student is expected to read aloud in the classroom in one minute. The *Study Programmes Guide for the Teacher* then translates the principles and objectives described in the study plan for basic education into a series of practical steps. There is one study programme for pre-primary education, one for each grade in primary education (covering the different educational fields) and one per subject within lower secondary education (covering all three grades) (i.e. the Reforma Integral de la Educación Básica; Fortoul, 2014).

A significant development in educational evaluation was the introduction in 2006 of the National Assessment of Academic Achievement in Schools (Evaluación Nacional del Logro Académico en Centros Escolares (ENLACE)) to measure student performance across the country. In basic education, this assessment was applied in each grade for grades 3 and above in Spanish and mathematics and a third subject which varied across years (e.g. history in 2010, geography in 2011). ENLACE's results were made public at the school level and had become an important tool to provide accountability to parents.

The Mexican framework for evaluation and assessment (see also OECD, 2012) consists of four components: student assessment, teacher appraisal, school evaluation and system evaluation. The first of these is student assessment. Student performances in Mexico are assessed by a wide range of instruments, ranging from national standardized assessments to continuous formative assessments in the classroom. Teachers assume the main responsibility for student assessments. All students are assessed in an ongoing manner throughout the school year in each curriculum area or subject. There are also externally based national final examinations at the end of both primary (Instrument for Testing New Lower Secondary School Students (IDANIS)) and lower secondary education (National Upper Secondary Education Entrance Exam (EXANI I)). These assessments serve diagnostic and selection (by school at the next level) purposes. As we have already suggested, at the national level, there was, though it has now been discontinued, a full-cohort external assessment (National Assessment of Academic Achievement in Schools (ENLACE)), which was used for diagnostic and improvement purposes but which also had 'high stakes' for teachers and schools.

Assessment can be low stakes or high stakes (see also Messick, 1989). ENLACE was initially presented as a low-stakes assessment, but it progressively evolved into a high-stakes examination. This is a consequence of other uses of its results, the most regressive being the utilization of student results in the National Teacher Career Programme (PNCM), so that a part of teachers' salaries was tied to their students' scores in ENLACE. Whilst ENLACE was used in the context of the PNCM since its inception in 2006, its original design was based on the formative use of its results for the improvement of teaching and learning in the classroom. Originally the SEP suggested the following low-stakes uses for ENLACE results: activities to involve parents in supporting their children's learning, such as workshops and reinforcement of learning at home; creating materials for improving teaching and promoting the exchange of experiences and good practices between teachers and states; the development of formative processes of learning based on ENLACE results; special initiatives to strengthen schools with low ENLACE results; actions for strengthening educational management, such as establishing learning standards at the end of each education level and promoting programmes for improving education quality.

But ENLACE rapidly became a high-stakes assessment with the publication of results at the school level, school rankings published in the media, monetary incentives for teachers based on their students' ENLACE scores and students with the highest scores receiving public recognition. These other uses of ENLACE were quite distinct from those initially intended; and they may have led schools, teachers and students to devote a large amount of time to practising ENLACE tests. The ENLACE programme was abolished in 2015.

The second component of the Mexican framework for evaluation and assessment is teacher appraisal (including school leader appraisal). Teacher appraisal is meant to be comprehensive and consists of a range of components covering the different stages of a teacher's career. There are examinations to select students into initial teacher education as well as diagnostic external examinations during and upon graduation from initial teacher education. Access to a permanent post is regulated through the National Teaching Post Competition, which, at present, is based on a standardized examination, the National Examination of Teaching Knowledge and Skills. Whilst in service the teacher can be appraised, on a voluntary basis, in three different situations: to access a promotion to a management post through the Vertical Promotion System (Escalafón Vertical); to access salary progression within each rank of the Vertical Promotion System through the National Teacher Career Programme (Programa Nacional de Carrera Magisterial); and to access collective and individual monetary rewards based on student standardized assessments results through the Incentives Programme for Teacher Quality (Programa de Estímulos a la Calidad Docente). In addition, the government is currently in the process of implementing a mandatory process of teacher appraisal covering all teachers, which is meant to be formative in nature, that is, the Universal Evaluation System (Evaluación Universal de Docentes). ENLACE results were heavily used in both the Universal Evaluation System and the National Teacher Career Programme. They were also used as the principal basis for the Incentives Programme for Teacher Quality.

The third element is school evaluation. There is no well-established, systematic approach to school evaluation. School-level aggregated data, including results in ENLACE assessments before the programme was discontinued, provide general information on student performance against state and national averages, but not in the context faced by schools. Schools are encouraged to engage in self-evaluation, and advice and instruments are provided nationally. Involvement is voluntary except in those cases where the school takes part in one of the federal education programmes, such as the Quality Schools Programme. No systematic external school evaluation exists.

The fourth component is system evaluation. The Secretariat of Public Education (SEP) is responsible for the overall monitoring and evaluation of the education system with the support of the National Institute for Educational Assessment and Evaluation (INEE). A range of tools is used to monitor performance of the education system. Information on student learning outcomes is collected from Educational Quality and Achievement Tests (EXCALE) at the end of pre-primary education and in grades 3, 6, 9 and 12 covering Spanish, mathematics, natural sciences and social sciences. The monitoring system also includes the collection of a range of statistics on education based on snapshot data collected from schools using a standardized format. These are the basis for annual publications with system-level indicators on education. International benchmarks of student performance provided by international student surveys such as PISA have been influential in driving policy development at the system level.

Assessments may be more or less integrated with the teaching programmes that pupils follow. Some kinds of assessment (for example, IQ tests) are not designed to measure pupil's learning (or the results of a teaching programme), in which case they are often associated with measures of qualities supposedly inherent in the student, such as intelligence. Assessment which is placed at the integrated end of the continuum is likely to be more informal than formal, more formative than summative, process- rather than product-orientated and to be frequent or continuous rather than taking place at one time point, usually at the end of the programme of study.

Summative assessments reflect the performance of a pupil at the end of a given period of instruction. These examinations are designed to assess the pupils' competences acquired over an extended period of time in a range of subjects. They are held under standardized physical conditions (relating to room arrangements, the use of specific formats, invigilation processes, etc.) and under time constraints. Formative modes of assessment are most closely associated with the process of teaching itself, but it is the results of these summative tests that are most visible and public. Formative dimensions of assessment focus on providing information for the teacher about the way learners complete particular tasks. The information provided is intended to feed directly into the teaching process, so the focus is on how students tackle these tasks and how they go about solving problems that they are given. The assessment environment does not need to be standardized during formative processes of assessment.

Summative assessment is concerned with determining whether students have mastered particular elements of the curriculum. It aims to be reliable and valid; and homogeneity of context is considered to be important so that comparability becomes possible. A summative assessment marks some point in the otherwise potentially organic teaching and learning process at which it is decided to stop teaching and give one's full attention to assessment. The stage at which it is most important to carry out this kind of assessment is often determined by factors other than those arising from learning goals, such as predetermined times in the school year or a requirement to report to other interested parties.

All the possible uses of assessment reflect decisions that have been made and will be made in the future about who and what is assessed, for what reason and in what way, and they all reflect a particular social context. The underlying principle when we are dealing with assessment practices is that educational assessment should be understood as a social practice. Although it is possible to trace policy issues in assessment back to the earliest days of public examinations – for example, when the Emperor Napoleon in France recognized the powerful contribution nationally controlled assessment procedures could play in cementing national unity – in recent years the importance of assessment as a policy tool has grown enormously as governments and education systems have come to realize its powerful potential as a mechanism of social control.

Assessment serves a wide range of purposes, ranging from the most commonplace of exchanges in a shop, for example, to school reports and high-stakes examinations, from individual job interviews to national monitoring. What unites all of these is the sense in which assessment first and foremost is a proxy for determining the quality of something or someone. It therefore operates as a mechanism for placing that person or object in a particular hierarchy of values, that is, comparing people with regards to a particular range of skills or rating a school more highly because its students have graduated with better examination results. Closely associated with this is the issue of legitimacy. The results of any particular assessment device have to be trusted by the public if the consequences are to be acceptable. Sadly, assessment issues are generally treated as technical matters, as focusing on improving the methodologies used to assess people rather than on the purposes or consequences of using such approaches, as in Mexico.

What this in effect means is that on occasions clear contradictions and tensions between common assessment practices emerge. An example of this in Mexico is the incompatibility between an increasingly test-driven educational and curricular culture and an explicit commitment to lifelong learning processes. Another example might be the tension between summative and formative purposes in an assessment process. This learning agenda, exemplified in the notion of formative assessment, is at odds with the use of punitive high-stakes testing, which has as its principle purpose raising standards, though the notion of a standard is in itself a contentious issue. Another tension within the system focuses on the more or less contradictory pressures of maintaining and even increasing enrolment whilst at the same time keeping standards high and ensuring that the public have confidence. Dore's (1976) now classic study of qualification inflation showed how the interaction between the supply of qualifications and the availability of employment opportunities tended to result in the pursuit of ever-higher levels of qualification as a form of educational inflation.

An important aspect of assessment is its increasing internationalization, exemplified by large-scale cross-national assessment studies, such as the Programme for International Student Assessment (PISA). What it is possible to argue is that there is now a world trade in educational policies, especially in relation to assessment issues. This policy borrowing, the take-up of apparently good ideas developed in one country by another, has further strengthened the grip of traditional assessment assumptions. Despite the significant evidence concerning flaws in international comparisons of student achievement, the power of the simple messages that can be and are derived from them has served to reinforce the prevailing domination of established forms of educational assessment.

Some of the defining aspects of recent assessment practices stand out with remarkable clarity. Chief among these is the increase in assessment activity of all kinds and the penetration of assessment in its various guises into almost every aspect of human endeavour. We have become assessment societies, as wedded to our belief in the power of numbers, grades, targets and league tables to deliver quality, accountability and equality as we are to modernism itself. History will readily describe the 1990s and 2000s 'the assessment eras', when belief in the power of assessment to provide a rational, efficient and publicly acceptable mechanism of judgement and control reached its high point across the world, and certainly in Mexico.

The assessment revolution has been one of scale, range and significance; a revolution that has elevated quantitative data, the raw material of most public assessments, as the principal mechanism for delivering transparency, accountability and predictability. The collection of data has become in itself a major instrument of social control, whether this is at the level of the individual, the institution or indeed a whole operational system such as in Mexico. All these various criticisms are helping to challenge the assumptions on which most of the existing edifices of assessment have been built. Belief in the power of conventional summative assessment techniques to be objective and efficient, to motivate present performance and to predict future performance, is being challenged by a range of research evidence that identifies significant flaws in these assumptions. Moreover, the assumptions highlight the worrying price that the use of assessment to measure and control extracts, including reduced motivation and significantly lower student performance.

Much of the familiar contemporary apparatus of assessment technologies was born of the modernist assumptions and educational needs of the nineteenth century. The assumptions informing these approaches can be identified as: the capacity to seek to identify relative levels of student performance as the basis for educational selection; to undertake such identification with a sufficient degree of objectivity that it provides a broadly fair outcome for the candidates affected; that the quality of such assessment is embodied in notions of reliability and validity; that students' scores on national examinations and tests provide a valid indicator of the quality of institutional performance; and that it is possible usefully to compare the productivity of individual education systems through international comparisons. Curriculum reforms in Mexico over the last 20 years have embraced and endorsed these assumptions. In the next chapter, we examine teacher-training practices across the states of Mexico.

4
Pre-Service and In-Service Training in Mexico

In this chapter, we examine the issue of teacher training, both pre- and in-service, and explore attempts to reform these important matters within the national context that concerns us, the Mexican education system. This means that any model of teacher learning environments that we might devise inevitably has to confront, and respond to, current arrangements and understandings of them. For example, the degree to which teacher-training institutions in Mexico have autonomy over their own curricula or the extent and type of in-service provision within the states are significant factors in the implementation of the model we argue for here.

We are concerned then, with professional learning environments and processes of professionalization, and how we can construct these, within the constraints and enablements of the teacher-training system in Mexico. Inevitably we are making judgements about a number of issues. These include the pedagogic mode (the type of relationship between the teacher-trainer and the student teachers), the learning mode (the type of learning approach that underpins the work of the teacher-trainer), the resources and technologies needed to allow that learning to take place, formative feedback mechanisms by the teacher-trainer (the modes, approaches and purposes), where the learning environment is, timings of different activities during the teaching sessions, the tasks that the student teachers are expected to complete, formative learning approaches (including assessment for learning approaches) and how the learning can be transferred to other environments. Learners here are student teachers and teachers already in service, and their learning environments are university and higher education institutions, schools and in-service training institutions in Mexico.

Models of teacher training

There are perhaps three dominant models of teaching and preparation for teaching: craftworker, executive technician and professional learner. We consider each of them before giving reasons for preferring the latter. Models are representations of the real world, without the extraneous detail. They are not the real world and it would be a mistake to think that they are. They are designed to help us better understand how the world works. However, their use raises a number of questions: for example, what representational purpose do they have? What kinds of entity are they? And what is their pedagogic function? In addition, any model that we articulate has normative elements, that is, we are explicitly suggesting that this model is better than other models that could be devised.

There are four ways of distinguishing between different models and judging that one is better than another. The first is epistemic: a model is superior to another because it is more empirically adequate. The second is the converse, so that a version of reality is better than another because it contains fewer contradictions, disjunctions and aporias. A third approach focuses on the giving of reasons, and concludes that some reasons and systems of rationality are superior to others, and therefore should be preferred. A fourth approach is pragmatic in a philosophical sense: a model is better than another because it is more practically adequate or referenced to/part of extant frameworks of meaning. Any successful model of the teacher-training curriculum and its associated pedagogies in Mexico therefore has to be more coherent, more empirically adequate, better referenced to frameworks of meaning and is underpinned by a more apt rationale than other models.

Craft knowledge has the following characteristics. It is rooted in practice and in the routines that shape practice, and this rules out certain types of learning or pedagogic approaches. This means that imitation and scaffolding various attempts to perform the activities are key to the development of this type of knowledge. The teacher or facilitator is the expert practitioner and knowledge is derived from exposure to the performances of the expert. The expert is therefore not primarily a skilled pedagogue but a skilled practitioner. The emphasis is placed on observing and imitating the practice. The justification for this is that the nature of the practice is better understood in these terms, that is, the learning object, becoming and being a good teacher, is a craft activity.

Craft knowledge values situated understanding and downplays the importance of technical know-how and critical reflection. This leaves little room for what might be called research-based knowledge, even if this is understood in a non-technicist way and as having a non-binding quality to it. Though advocates of craft-based knowledge accept that there may be a role for systematic propositional knowledge, this is confined to what is taught, or subject-based knowledge, rather than to the processes of teaching and learning that the teacher or student teacher is engaged in. Furthermore, this entails a clear separation between content and process knowledge or between the learning object and the pedagogic process. In addition, this focus on practical judgements as the essence of the teaching activity fails to account for ethical and epistemological elements in the judgements teachers make. These judgements as a consequence of their lack of reflective critique and adherence to external expert judgement may be conservative and potentially unreliable, based as they are on observations of existing practice and common popularizations.

The second of our teaching models is the executive technician. This requires the teacher to perform in a particular way: to have, and be able to execute, a repertoire of pre-conceived actions. In this model, teaching is a rule-based activity and learning is understood as the assimilation of these rules and ways of enacting them, without recourse to critical reflection or situated understanding. The executive technician model (see also Winch, 2014) recognizes the value of research findings, and this means that it is not thought appropriate for teachers to interpret those findings for themselves. Mexican educational researchers generate findings which can be expressed as protocols for action, and the role of the teacher is to implement these protocols in the most efficient way possible given that there are always situational constraints. One consequence of this is that the knowledge which is being transferred tends to lack a sense of change, emergence, immediacy or relevance. This positions the learning object, these rules and protocols, outside space and time and effectively reifies it. This also applies to the assimilative and performative functions of learning.

These rules are identified by researchers and practical policymakers as external to the setting. They are not situation specific or even sensitive to the particularities of the setting in which they are being applied. Educational research is understood as the making of nomothetic statements about educational activities; educational disputes about how teachers should behave in the classroom are settled by atheoretical and value-free empirical enquiry and theoretical knowledge of educational matters is thought of as superior to practical knowledge. As a result, practice is understood as the efficient application of theoretical knowledge constructed by professional experts. Learning at pre-service and in-service levels then is reduced to the assimilation of these rules and to ways of following them in concrete situations such as classrooms. A more refined version of the executive technician model is that educational propositional knowledge should not be understood as being applicable in every possible circumstance and as having a certainty of outcome, but it can act as a guide to practical action. This brings back a measure of interpretative activity into the proceedings.

Both the craft and executive technician models can be contrasted with a professional learning model. Professional learning emanates and is derived from an understanding of the characteristics and functions of being a classroom teacher in the context of where that teaching takes place, in this case, Mexico. Apart from the content and methodological knowledge that teachers need in order to plan and teach a lesson, they also have to take a variety of other factors into consideration and integrate them in a coherent, efficient and pedagogically effective way. Among these are the previous knowledge, schooling biographies and expectations of their students, the individual differences between them (e.g. capabilities, interests and motivations), the objectives of the programme and the overall institution, as well as their own pedagogical aims, theoretical assumptions and values. Teachers have to make a considerable number of instantaneous and ad hoc decisions. They need to react to and take the lead in classroom interactions and modify their plans and methodological procedures according to the needs of students at specific points during the lesson. Ideally, they should create an atmosphere that encourages learning and communication and make sure that the task level is neither too high nor too low. In addition to this, institutions as well as classes have their own particular norms and patterns of interaction and communication. Teachers play a key role in mediating between this institutional culture and their students. They usually determine the content of classroom talk, organize the distinct phases of the lesson, determine the behaviour that is expected from students, select who is permitted to respond to a question or contribute to a discussion, decide what kind of answers are regarded as valid and so forth.

The fact that teachers have to take a multitude of sequential and simultaneous decisions which have to take account of personal, interpersonal, interactive, disciplinary, pedagogic and institutional factors requires a new approach to in-service teacher training and development. Imposing a pre-defined and fixed innovation on teachers (and students) in diverse institutional and regional contexts in a coercive, top-down fashion is counterproductive and likely to make them revert to safe and routinized practices. It seems more promising to encourage practitioners to try out new ideas in their classroom, to make adjustments and then justify their decisions. To this end an awareness of the contexts teachers work in and their own behavioural and communicative patterns is developed. Participants analyse their own classes, strengthen their communicative competences and classroom management strategies, and amplify their pool of teaching resources.

Donald Schon, in his seminal work *The Reflective Practitioner* (2005), focused on how practitioners operate and learn in workplace settings. He suggested that most of our knowledge as it relates to action, or knowledge-in-action, is implicit. It does not involve conscious processes, so that actions, recognitions and judgements are skilled activities carried out spontaneously. Equally implicit is the knowledge the practitioner holds about the background, the history and the social embeddedness of the respective practice. This might lead one to conclude that professional action is basically a problem-solving activity where reflection and existing tacit knowledge is applied to emerging problems. Schon however argued that this widespread understanding of professional practice is too limited and has to be extended to problem setting, a more complex form of reflection, where the practitioner considers wider concerns and implications of the problem. These include institutional, political and social structures external to the workplace itself (in our particular case, the classroom) but which impact on it. At this stage, the practitioner sets in motion a process of renaming and reframing of the problem. Indeed, he or she might not even consider the issue at hand to be a problem anymore; though it is more likely that this meta-process will provide the learner with a different type of problem requiring a different type of solution.

Reflexivity and conscious analysis become even more necessary when the professional is confronted with new situations and as a consequence, has to change or acquire new practices. Though the individual perceives the new situation to be unique in the first instance, to make sense of it requires its assimilation into existing frameworks of rules and resources. People do this by looking for similarities and differences. Schon understood the process of learning as cyclical with successive iterations of comparing new and familiar experiences with well-established routines of thinking, many of which the learner (in our case the teacher-practitioner) may have difficulty with bringing to consciousness. In professional practice, however, the individual also interacts with and acts upon the environment. They attempt to make sense of it in an experimental fashion that involves the following non-sequential processes: exploring the possibilities inherent in the problem; developing a series of action steps; testing them out to see if they fit the problem; and evaluating the more successful solutions to develop working hypotheses. Experimenting in practice then is both reflective and transactional. The teacher is at the same time testing out new hypotheses and seeking to change the external setting in which the problem is embedded.

Professional development in this model is therefore a process of reflection in action, with different degrees of complexity, and reflection on action, where teachers have to be encouraged to experiment with and explore new practices, contents and procedures in their actual workplace contexts and to think about their relevance, usefulness and viability. Reflection however, can be greatly increased through collaborative meaning making, dialogue and discussion between different practitioners who can add alternative perspectives, ideas and experiences. The exchanges between teachers from the same or different schools provide a further level of reflexivity to the teacher development programme, namely reflection on reflection in and on action.

Teacher-training practices

One of the key issues with teacher-training practices is the extent and type of collaboration between teacher-training institutions in Mexico and Mexican schools (see also Maandag et al., 2007). These teacher-training institutions are understood as universities, colleges of higher education and any formal body that provides and accredits teacher training that is separate from the practice sites. Maandag and his colleagues (2007) developed a fivefold model to explain this relationship. The first model is a work placement model. Here most of the training activity takes place at the teacher-training institutions and members of these organizations have full control over the programme being offered. The second model they propose is a coordinator model, where most of the training activities take place at the teacher-training institution; however, the school takes on the responsibility of coordinating, and to some extent delivering, the supervision of the student teachers in the schools. The third model is a partnership model, and here training activities are shared between the teacher-training provider and the school. The school provides instruction in the subjects to be taught and in the most appropriate pedagogical strategies, and the school provides placement opportunities, practice *in situ* and some evaluative activity about the performance of the student. The fourth model is a network framework, and here training activities are shared between the teacher-training institution and the school. The duties of each are very similar; however, there is a much more intensive relationship between the two, with tutors moving between and operating at both sites. The fifth model is a training school model, in which all the training takes place in the school. In this model, the teacher-training institution can be thought of as a reserve and reinforcement body, undertaking some training of the school and school-based tutors and developing teaching and training methods. In some scenarios, the teacher-training institution disappears altogether.

The five models allocate different roles and responsibilities between the teacher-training institution and the school, with the first and last of these models representing scenarios in which one or other of the two providers, the teacher-training institution and the school, have almost complete control over the contents, organization and accreditation of the programme. In the third and fourth models, there is greater pedagogical and curricular collaboration between the school and the teacher-training institution, although the extent and nature of this collaboration may vary considerably depending on the individual programme. For novice teachers, there may be less of a distinction between different elements of the programme or different sites of formation in the fourth model than in the other models, whereas for the first and last models processes of formation may be experienced as either institutional-or school-based.

Initial teacher training can be organized in two ways. In the concurrent model, academic subjects are studied alongside educational and professional studies throughout the duration of the course. An example of this is the Mexican Bachelor of Education programme. This kind of programme has several benefits; and in particular, it allows a more integrated learning experience, since pedagogical training and subject-matter (content knowledge) training take place at the same time. These kinds of programmes can also have disadvantages; notably, they are less flexible than consecutive models, since the students are required to decide if they want to become a teacher at a very early stage in their university studies. If teacher-training is accessible only through concurrent programmes, it can create difficulties to becoming a teacher for those who have studied something other than education in the first place, as well as for those who are interested in becoming teachers, but who might also want to re-enter other labour markets eventually.

In the consecutive model, the specialized courses in pedagogy and in teaching are accessible after having completed another degree in a discipline taught in school (teachers are educated first in a specific discipline and then they receive pedagogical training). This model is more common for senior schoolteachers than for basic-level schoolteachers. Its main advantage lies in the fact that it allows a flexible entry into teacher training. Indeed, since the aspirant teachers already have another degree, they can convert themselves more easily if their interests or job perspectives change. This flexibility also makes them better equipped if there is a change in labour market conditions. In some subjects, it is essential for the teacher to have a strong subject expertise that can sometimes be achieved only due to prior studies in that specific field (for example, in mathematics or history). The negative aspect of such an initial teacher-training programme is that teachers formed through the consecutive model can have a weaker knowledge in learning techniques and in pedagogy in general. Since they have studied in two different cycles, where they learned two different aspects of teaching, their learning process is fragmented rather than integrated.

In an education system, both consecutive and concurrent models can coexist. There are advantages and disadvantages to this coexistence. Having several programmes of initial teacher training attracts into the profession different types of potential teachers, and this is particularly important in a country such as Mexico that has in the past faced teacher shortages. Indeed, concurrent model programmes attract students that feel they have a teaching vocation, and consecutive model programmes allow the aspirant teacher to first study something else, before undertaking a programme of teacher training. Having several teacher-training programmes, based on different models, can represent an extra cost to the country and be less efficient.

In general terms, entry into concurrent education programmes is based on secondary school results and entry into consecutive courses depends on the results of university studies. In some countries, there is strong competition to enrol on teacher education programmes; in others teaching as a career is considered to be a fallback position, in that it was considered to be a second or even third option on graduation from the university. In Mexico, this latter position is more likely to be the reality.

The length of the period of initial teacher training varies round the world between a three-year period to, in some countries, six years. In the latter case, an important consideration is the capacity to conduct and use research, both *in situ* and elsewhere. There are elements of this in all teacher-training programmes round the world. Schwille and Dembélé (2007) suggest that there are many factors that have to be taken into account by policymakers when deciding the length of initial teacher training: economic constraints, the potential shortage or abundance of teachers, the amount and quality of teacher candidates' content knowledge, their capacity for pedagogical knowledge and the state of the labour market in general.

One of the most recent and important trends in teacher education is the development of alternative pathways into the teaching profession. These programmes have been developed in situations of teacher shortage; their main purpose is to increase the supply of teachers in areas of need, geographical or relative to a particular subject (IT, languages, mathematics, etc.). It is possible to highlight several characteristics that define this model: the programme is short, and the preparation is mainly organized through practical training. Also, a low priority is given to educational theory and research and to scientific knowledge. They rely on the candidates' previous education to provide adequate grounding in the subject matter. The curriculum itself emphasizes learning by doing. Another common form of continuing training is the cascade model; a select group of teachers are trained and are then expected to transmit the ideas at the school level to other teachers. This form of continuing training usually occurs when the educational authorities' principal concern is to reach as many participants as possible in a short time, and on a short budget, for example, with indigenous populations in Mexico.

Teacher training

For both initial and later in-service training, the institutions the government set up were largely concerned with producing so-called conveyors of the national ethic. The emphasis was not on subjects and learning. The institutions themselves, generically referred to as *Escuelas Normales*, existed under a variety of names: Escuelas Normales Rurales, Escuelas Rurales Regionales or Centrales Agrícolas, Escuelas Regionales Campesinas, Escuela Normal de Profesores de Instrucción Primaria, Escuela Normal Superior de Mexico, Escuela Nacional de Maestros, Escuela Nacional de Educadores, Centros Normales Regionales and Benemérita Escuela Nacional de Maestros. They were all tightly regulated by the central government with a strong input from the SNTE. Universities until recent times did not participate in the training of teachers largely because they were considered to be unreliable, despite the fact that they could offer a higher quality education than that provided by the centrally controlled institutions. Even the Universidad Pedagógica Nacional (UPN) was strictly regulated.

The result was a poor quality education for aspiring teachers and this translated into a poor education for children. Only in more recent times when the link between economic and social development and education was recognized were the bonds relatively and reluctantly loosened. On paper, the current teacher-training curriculum appears to measure up to the best practices at the international level, and to be based on the view long held by international organizations and agencies that teachers need to have both the support and the freedom to be creative and to adapt their knowledge to the needs and possibilities of their students. The teacher-training curriculum in the Mexican teacher-training colleges now incorporates pedagogical subject-based knowledge and training in decision making. These aspects therefore explicitly mark it off from the older prescriptive approach, in which social control rather than the acquisition and application of knowledge, skills and dispositions was the guiding principle. In theory, by the end of the four-year course the student teacher should have acquired the specific capacities to teach, a solid grounding in their subject, the ability to impart that knowledge, a set of professional ethics, and an ability to understand the students' circumstances and characteristics and be able to respond to them creatively. The work set up to develop this profile is divided into five blocks: pedagogical skills and historical and social contexts, subject knowledge, a specialist option, ICT and a second language, and teaching practice.

It has been far from easy putting the new curriculum into practice. Two recurrent tensions in teacher training over the years since the Mexican Revolution have influenced its evolution or more accurately, led to its stagnation. The first of these is the tension between the teacher as street bureaucrat or foot soldier for nationalism and the autonomous professional. If the latter is in the ascendancy, there are still siren voices that insist on control, tradition and conformity, with decision-makers and teachers themselves clinging to the old view as loyal subjects and conveyers of national values.

In addition, the new curriculum is replete with internal inconsistencies. Both the 1997 and 2012 initial teacher-training programmes made great play of contextualizing the curriculum in relation to what they called a diversity of cultures, an emphasis on social background and how it affected individual performance and the enormous disparity between facilities offered in schools. Nevertheless, as Fortoul (2014) points out, the 2012 reform package sidelined these issues by choosing to foreground the psycho-pedagogical or universal human aspects of learning over and against the different ways that students learn as a result of their different socio-economic-cultural backgrounds. This shift, that was never explained, made it difficult for teachers to make sense of what they had learnt when it came to teaching basic and universal concepts in the classroom. For example, notions of counting and measuring are different in different parts of the country due to different cultural interpretations of these concepts. With regards to language matters, the teachers encountered even more difficulties.

Ruth Mercado (2010) has argued persuasively that teacher training should serve the school rather than the school serving and conforming to the teacher-training regime. This cogent and telling criticism might well be extended to most aspects of how educational policy is fashioned and delivered in Mexico. In addition to the inconsistency resulting from the imposition of generalized pedagogical principles in very different learning conditions, current teacher training has been mired in a long tradition of prescription and reliance on inappropriate mechanisms to achieve those ends. The 1997 reforms and its 2012 successor have made bold attempts to depart from the idea that teachers are merely conveyers of officially sanctioned knowledge in its gestures towards inculcating what they call generative abilities or competences for teachers and young learners. Commentators have lamented the continued reluctance or, perhaps, inability of teachers' colleges to generate reflection and collective and dialogical learning, in spite of paying lip service to these notions.

Recent studies point out that trainee teachers say they benefit from the increased contact with schools in the last two semesters as well as the introduction of practical exercises with their peers (for example, Instituto Nacional para la Evaluación de la Educación, 2016). From the evidence, it is clear that the link personnel in the college and the host school play a key role in the success of this exercise. This lynchpin of teaching practice varies between the institutions and states. Especially in more remote and poorer areas of large cities and in rural and/or predominately indigenous areas, the services of local support teachers and their linkages with the teachers' colleges may be weak or non-existent. As it is often the case with programmes needing administrative coordination, there is little support or monitoring of teaching practice.

Remedi (1999, 135) also alerts us to the way learning in teacher-training colleges is reduced to simple predigested prescriptions. He suggests that teacher-trainers:

> dismiss the teachers' enquiries and replace them with pre-set models and recipes, masquerading as authoritative representations of the world around them, based on generalities, rules and laws that give a sense or order to the chaos they imagine exists. These teaching experts roll on from one conjuncture to the next one, with the certainty of possessing the truth; in this facade, they seduce the

teachers with a series of norms set in models of what should be, and recipes that slip pass the official gaze and stops the teachers from basing them on a solid academic foundation.

The full implications of this only become evident when the student teachers make contact with the pupils in the schools.

At the outset of their careers, novice teachers encounter a number of difficulties in fulfilling their pedagogical duties. The most obvious of these is time constraints. For many decades now, studies have shown that it is difficult if not impossible to cover adequately the basic education curricula (for example, Martin, 2004). Even a cursory glance at the programmes for the primary and secondary levels shows that the contents and the didactics that the current competences-based approach demands require the equivalent of a full school day, that is the norm in other countries, but not in Mexico.

In-service training

It is not our intention to explore the often meticulously prepared and crafted in-service training programmes for practising teachers, advisors, evaluators and administrators whose pedagogy in the majority of cases is based on the principle of learning as problem-solving. Our aim is to look at the way institutional derangements can distort or even prevent such courses, programmes and workshops from being effective and, in some cases, from taking place. The fault is not in the design or the commitment of the designers but in the incoherent, contradictory and paralysing system of delivery that we have referred to previously.

The origins of in-service training lie in attempts to consolidate and regularize the expansion of education that took place during the 1930s, in part, through the mobilization and enthusiasm of the Socialist Education Movement. By the 1940s the education authorities were confronted with the double problem of developing a qualified and expanding corps of teachers and bringing what they saw as institutional order into educational programmes and institutions. Many practising and committed teachers particularly in rural areas had few if any formal qualifications; these teachers had played an active part in the Socialist Education Movement that they viewed as an extension of the political revolution. They aspired to provide coverage throughout the country in line with one of the key promises of the revolution. These largely self-taught and highly motivated teachers, reminiscent of organizations like the nineteenth-century Irish hedge schools and the teachers' brigades that were organized in the aftermath of the Russian Revolution, worked impossibly long days. In the morning, they taught children in whatever premises could be commandeered given the lack of school buildings and facilities. In the afternoon, they organized and fronted adult literacy programmes for parents and at weekends, they arranged special courses largely designed to provide women with the knowledge, skills and dispositions to take their rightful place as producers in and full members of the community. For these teachers, learning how to read and write was inseparable from aspiring to a new social order, and their texts and classes were built round encouraging their students to develop their own views. In brief, they sought to imbue literacy and the vocational with political awareness and expression. However, this came into conflict with the Partido de la Revolución Mexicana (PRM) that saw itself as the sole arbiter of what should be, and how it should be, taught.

In formal terms these teachers were largely unqualified. It was estimated that in 1941 76 per cent of teachers in the federal system and 86 per cent of rural teachers were without training. In 1945 only 50 per cent of existing teachers had finished primary school, only 19 per cent had entered the secondary system and only another 19 per cent had successfully trained at rural teacher-training institutions (see also Santillán, 2012). The matter of control that so worried the PRM was put firmly on the agenda in 1940 when General Manuel Ávila Camacho succeeded the more socially minded and innovative Lázaro Cárdenas to the presidency. Ávila Camacho described teachers who participated in politics as 'outlaws'. A campaign of 'regularization' was launched which in 1942 led to the establishment of the Escuela Normal Superior de México as a four-year post-upper secondary and teacher-training establishment. As Marcela Santillán (2012, 46) has pointed out, here the tendency was to concentrate less on the quality of academic training than 'to control the political participation of the teaching profession' and educate teachers to be 'technicians of instruction'. This objective was further elaborated on by the then Minister of Education, Jaime Torres Bodet. His idea was to rein in the activities of the teachers. The aim of these establishments, he maintained, was to equip teachers with '. . . a series of useful and simple rules, some simple formulae to learn and retain in order to improve their techniques and provide advice about physical and moral health' (Santillán, 2012, 46).

To that effect, in 1945 he set up the Instituto Federal de Capacitación del Magisterio to offer correspondence courses leading to certification. Over the years it became apparent that teachers were receiving a poor education at the teacher-training colleges. This led to the establishment of the multi-campus Universidad Pedagógica Nacional (UPN) in 1978, which was set up, in part at the behest of the teachers' trade union, to grant degrees in education and to serve as a model and a yardstick. According to official figures (see also Secretaría de Educación Pública, 2014), between 1940 and 1952 the number of teachers increased by just under 67 per cent and the number of schools by just under 16 per cent. Moreover, the ministry had little knowledge of the teachers they employed and of their trainers in the training colleges. As a first step, it was decided to gather information. Hence, somewhat belatedly in 1954 the Junta Nacional de Educación Normal was asked to undertake a general review of the system, gather profiles of the teachers and revise teaching programmes.

Whilst considerable attention was given to the curriculum for teacher training between 1942 and 1972, as Isaias Alvarez (2002) points out, the piecemeal approach to in-service training continued. In 1971 the Dirección General de Mejoramiento Profesional del Magisterio (later called the Dirección General de Capacitación y Mejoramiento Profesional del Magisterio (DGMPM)) was created to upgrade the teachers in pre-primary, primary and secondary schools. Despite the efforts of this new institution, sufficient funds were not made available to allow it to develop sufficient courses to fill the gap. In the same year an educational research centre, the Departamento de Investigaciones Educativas (DIE), was set up as part of the Centro de Investigación y de Estudios Avanzados del Instituto Politécnico Nacional (CINESTAV) under the leadership of Juan Manuel Gutiérrez Vásquez and Olac Fuentes Molinar. It too was at first unable to obtain support to combine research with learning. Many of the staff led by Gutiérrez Vásquez therefore worked with non-governmental institutions.

That is, in-service programmes were not given a high priority, until in 1984 the government decreed that all entrants to teacher-training colleges had to have a school-leaving certificate as a result of the 1982 decision to upgrade the status of teacher-training schools to that of higher education institutions. The suddenness of this new requirement meant that enrolment declined precipitously. Only after the event within the labyrinthine components of the ministry was it suggested that the absence of relevant in-service programmes could have lessened or even prevented a shortage of qualified teachers. As Marcela Santillán (2012) commented, the administration and organization could not cope with their existing responsibilities and duties let alone take on new ones. It was not until 1989, as a result of what was called a national consultation for the modernization of education, that in-service training was placed firmly on the agenda. The consultation in its recommendations concluded by stating that there was a pressing need to establish a pertinent, efficient and permanent system for in-service training.

Meanwhile, so severe was the problem of retention that divisions of the ministry such as curriculum development stepped in and began to provide short programmes in areas of expertise in order to update the skills of teachers and provide them with new pedagogic methods. Liaison between the federal government, the states and most stakeholder organizations was so poor at this stage that to do this it was necessary to create an unofficial network of advisors throughout the country to override existing institutions. For example, an effective network of mathematicians set up programmes with the help of well-established research organizations like the Departamento de Investigaciones Educativas (DIE) of the Centro de Investigación y de Estudios Avanzados del Instituto Politécnico Nacional (CINESTAV) led by Eugenio Filloy Yagüe, Elisa Bonilla Rius and Hugo Balbuena Corro in the SEP. Something more permanent than dependence on individuals was required.

For this reason, three years later in 1992 the recommendations of the 1989 consultation exercise led to the establishment of a curriculum to develop existing staff through the Programa Emergente de Actualización del Magisterio and the Programa de Actualización de Maestros. Despite the relatively short life of these programmes, for the first time they laid the basis for the construction of a national policy. In 1994, after the signing of the Acuerdo Nacional para la Modernización de la Educación Básica and after an agreement on how to share responsibilities between the federal and state ministries of education, the SEP and the SNTE fleshed out the basic guidelines of the Programa Nacional para la Actualización Permanente de los Maestros de Educación Básica (PRONAP). In essence, whilst each state was to be responsible for the planning and administration of education, the federal government still retained full control over the curriculum, and hence continued to intervene at all levels in its delivery. In 1995, with the signing of a series of agreements between the federal government and the states along these lines, the PRONAP came into effect.

It led to the creation of teachers' centres in states where they had not previously existed. Some 266 Centros de Maestros for training through workshops and national courses came into existence. In 1997 these activities were combined with appraisal processes. In 2003 PRONAP became an instrument for assigning resources to the states for a new policy of in-service training. In 2005 the Dirección General de Formación Continua de Maestros en Servicio (DGFCMS) was created within the federal ministry with the task of providing technical support to the states, as well as establishing in-service training centres under its guidance and evaluating the work undertaken in these centres.

An enormous pot-pourri of courses, seminars and workshops was created in a disorganized and uncoordinated manner. Most states took advantage of the financial support offered by the federal government to devise courses some of which only ever existed on paper. One of the problems was that many of the state ministries had never had proper research and development sections and even where they existed they were populated by trade-union-sponsored teachers '*en comisión*', as federal officials soon found out. Many states lacked trained personnel and because there was rarely anything like a working relationship and/or a mechanism for collaboration, they either ran few courses or had to request help from the ministry. The ministry was in no position to respond to their requests. The federal ministry itself had little or no knowledge of who ran which courses and where they took place, if indeed they took place at all. The federal ministry contributed to the confusion because, as we have seen, many of its own divisions had set up their own courses run by experts in collaboration with carefully selected teams in the provinces, much to the chagrin of state and trade-union authorities. These often-excellent courses, workshops and seminars were in many cases in competition with those set up by the new DGFCMS. Teachers never knew if a course would be recognized or even take place. The teachers' centres were ill-equipped to set up, run and evaluate courses. There was no clear and consistent division of labour within the institutions and even less between them.

The DGFCMS set itself the unrealistic task of bringing the smorgasbord of what was on offer under its wings. They did not take into account the ongoing work of other sections of the ministry nor did they have sufficient knowledge of what was going on in individual states. Their aim was to organize the states so that they offered in-service training for all subjects, pedagogy, information technology, school management and so on through a modular system set up, managed and accredited centrally. The idea was to manage if not micromanage almost 600 programmes offered to over a million teachers and to provide appropriate certification. These courses were to be run through the 574 Centros de Maestros established throughout the country (see also Secretaría de Educación Pública, 2014). These institutions, too, varied enormously in quality and reach, with some being little more than paper institutions. Just under half were located in 9 of the 32 states and these states tended to monopolize the offer. Needless to say, the poorest states with the least developed educational infrastructure were those that participated the least in the in-service programme. The ministry itself recognized that some of the teacher centres were populated with advisors and assessors from different national programmes that often overlapped whilst others suffered from a shortage of personnel.

Nevertheless, the ministry personnel, largely drawn from universities like the UPN, were determined to deal with the general problem and also with what they saw as one of the great obstacles to the effectiveness of the system, the lack of training in the increasingly important areas of administration, organization and leadership. Their first step was to collect information about the field and to see if they could use an already existing structure to begin to work towards a more coherent system of organization. However, many states had never conducted a proper audit, others refused to provide information or provided information that was difficult to interpret and teacher organizations responsible for large numbers of teachers and administrators '*en comisión*' blocked attempts to gather basic information.

Designing in-service training courses

To illustrate the difficulties in designing courses for in-service training and making them both viable and sustainable, we trace the history of one such initiative from its conception, through its planning and to its implementation. It will show the enormous institutional obstacles that made it difficult to put into effect in-service training for educators and administrators. It was decided that a group of advisors called Asesores Técnicos Pedagógicos (ATPs) appointed by both federal and state authorities could be the key to innovation within schools and between schools, authorities and parents. The ATPs were involved in a multitude of activities that included promoting educational policies, organizing courses, seminars and workshops for teachers, directors, supervisors and administrative staff, fostering innovation in the curriculum and ways of teaching, and serving as a liaison between the home and the school. Many also ran local teaching centres. However, their roles were ill-defined. It was felt that if they could begin to see themselves as a coherent and effective body with an esprit de corps and if they were provided with proper training, they could serve as a catalyst to improve the work within schools and perhaps begin to use the school as the heart of a programme for community development.

The institutional origin of the initiative stemmed from the fact that the education departments of universities shied away from research and training initiatives in primary education. Their research efforts were almost exclusively focused on investigations in higher education. Moreover, the Universidad Pedagógica Nacional created to service the teaching profession lacked the influence to deliver these new initiatives. The state universities did not have the day-to-day experience of the various branches of the UPN to be involved in delivering courses. It was reasoned that collaboration between the UPN and a state university that had an extramural department like the Universidad Autónoma Metropolitana-Xochimilco could successfully provide both research and training to a high level. Moreover, it was further thought that the newly created Coordinación General de Educación Intercultural y Bilingüe could help mould the courses to the needs and possibilities of the hitherto neglected indigenous communities.

The first step was to identify the constituency. The process took a year of delicate negotiations with state authorities and state affiliates of the SNTE because there was no real comprehensive record of how many ATPs there were and what functions they had. Information could not be obtained from all the states because some, for largely political reasons, refused to disclose the data, if indeed they possessed it. Some data could only be collected at second hand through the goodwill of local contacts. What emerged was a profile that showed that ATPs were largely unqualified for this type of work. The skills and academic backgrounds ranged from doctoral level to a large number with little or no teacher training. In some states, they acted as advisors and liaison officers and in others, seemed to have no function at all except that of running the local teacher centres.

An interdisciplinary team consisting of the Coordinacion General de Actualizacion y Capacitacion para Maestros en Servicio (CGAyCMS) staff, the DIE, UAM, UPN, Coordinación General de Educación Bilingüe y Intercultural, CONAFE and representatives of ATPs from two states was assembled. Negotiations were conducted with all the stakeholders: the federal authorities, the state authorities, existing organizations that were promoting such activities, the ATPs themselves, the political organizations, the trade unions at the federal and state level, and established interest groups at all levels of the ministry itself. The process was protracted, with each interest group able to intervene at any stage of the proceedings.

The courses were ambitious in their scope, aims and methodology built round the premises of action research. In essence, they were designed to equip the advisors with an ability to: monitor and evaluate the schools, their culture, their teachers and locate problems to be solved by all within the school; assess and support the schools, teachers and administrators to plan courses based on needs and possibilities and school and community environments, and to promote group problem-solving; mediate relations between schools and authorities by first being provided with an understanding of the state and federal systems and being equipped with design strategies, and to encourage collaborative work by promoting educationalists to reflect upon work problems and to devise possible solutions. At the heart of the strategy was the idea of involving all levels of the organization in the attempt to find solutions, working together to overcome the hierarchical problems that had impeded change in the past and, more importantly, involving the community in all stages of work in the schools.

One set of problems arose from the fact that the chosen institutions of higher education found it difficult intellectually and institutionally to collaborate and slowly moved from working together to setting up their own courses. It proved to be a Sisyphean struggle for the universities, which slowly retreated from the action research model that they had originally proposed into the more reassuring one: curriculum with a traditional pedagogy, similar to the short-term, decontextualized, predigested recipe courses given by private institutions. In the end, the courses were designed by ministry personnel, who also delivered them. Another set of problems was created by the very different backgrounds of potential participants, who were selected by the state authorities. Some states chose not to participate and not all the states, which had made the decision to be part of the programme, used the same criteria for selection. In most cases the criteria had more to do with their political stance than with knowledge and need. Moreover, the ministry personnel had to carefully negotiate the contents of the courses with local authorities, the trade unions and other stakeholders. Finally, the ATPs found that when they tried to initiate programmes based on the courses, they were usually prevented from doing so by state authorities and the state teacher federations. The courses were popular and provided those ATPs who attended them with the relevant diplomas they required to recoup their expenses and inspired some to undertake research degrees. Because of the multiple layers of negotiation, the rigidness of structures and the lack of institutional change, much to the frustration of the teams who spent several years researching and preparing the programmes, they rarely met their aims.

We have seen that there was a demonstrable need for in-service training to upgrade teachers and administrators and to provide them with the tools to better accomplish their jobs. Excellent programmes and innovative approaches were devised to allow them to develop their skills and, in the case of the ATPs, to serve as an effective and inventive liaison between the school and the community. The sticking point has been that almost every new initiative led to the creation of new institutions that not only did not replace already existing institutions but also overlapped with them, to such an extent that territorial conflicts resulted. Similarly, state authorities had the power to block new initiatives without being able to develop alternatives. As Marcela Santillán (2012) points out, the existing tension between the federal and state governments became a 'permanent source of conflict'. The result was too many institutions crowding the field, each with the ability to block the others. Adding for the first time in 2008 institutions of higher education, in particular private universities, to the list of possible providers of in-service training courses did not improve the situation.

This method, that leads inevitably to blockages and insurmountable obstacles, is the rule and not an aberration. Every institutional arrangement or structure communicates a message, as Lévi-Strauss and Marcel Mauss pointed out long ago. In this case the message is that change is rarely successful. The effect on teachers who already were subject to a plethora of directives and programmes was to confirm them in their passive resistance. Parents noted the broken promises and in a country where education was always seen as the most important product of the revolution, they became increasingly sceptical, and if they could, they opted out of the system. The returning ATPs invigorated by their courses were unable to initiate meaningful change within their institutions. Meanwhile, teacher-training colleges were still not permitted to develop research and extension services. Overall the form devalued the content.

In this chapter, we have identified three models of teacher training: craft-based approaches, executive technician approaches and professional learning approaches. We have also seen how elements of the professional learning approach have influenced the policies and practices of teacher education in Mexico over the last 50 years. However, it is our contention that many of the benefits of this approach have been lost in the politics and maladministration of the system during this period of time. Another element of an education system is the role and influence parents might have. In the next chapter, we examine this important issue.

5

Parents and the Mexican Education System

Having examined attempts to reform the curriculum and pedagogy and the training of teachers, we now turn our attention to the roles played by parents in Mexico. In this chapter, we suggest that even the best intentioned and crafted of innovations sometimes conflict with the systems of control and that the system itself encourages parents to abstain from participating in the education of their children.

One of the key points of the Programa de Modernización de la Educación 1989–94, given lawful status in the 1993 Ley General de Educación, and the 1995 Programa de Desarrollo Educativo 1995–2000, was to strengthen and/or create appropriate mechanisms to encourage and allow parents to be more directly involved in the day-to-day education of their children. The ruling party, the teachers' trade union and the government were alarmed at what they perceived to be a significant and long-term deterioration in the relationship between parents and schools. Early in 1993 the Union Nacional de Padres de Familia publicly chastised the government for not taking into account the views of parents. By that time large sections of the urban middle class had deserted the state system of education. The poor, rural and indigenous populations, normally unconditional supporters of the system, had lost faith in the school to deliver as promised. Moreover, the authorities were aware that the growing scepticism of the population could result in civil unrest if they were to make public the information they had gathered that showed how poorly the schools were performing. They therefore resorted to the tried-and-tested corporativist strategy of attempting to incorporate potential critics into the system by providing them with a mechanism that superficially appeared to be a way to channel their criticisms, ideas and opinions. This time-honoured top-down procedure of adapting and modifying, in this case the policy of parental involvement in school governance, was intended to disarm critics.

The government felt that the 1974 Programa de Orientación Educativa a Padres de Familia was inadequate to the task. Its provisions spelled out in detail parental responsibility for the education of their children without providing a conduit for making their voices heard in the school and with local education authorities to begin to play a role in the modification of their modus operandi. The 1993 Ley General de Educación was designed to bring about greater parental and community participation in schooling. The new law established the basis for what were called Consejos Escolares de Participación Social en la Educación (commonly known by its acronym CEPS). The essence of CEPS was that for the first time parents would be part, albeit in a limited way, of the decision-making processes that included the promotion of learning and good behaviour, making technological improvements to the school infrastructure and the fostering of extra-curricular activities (Secretaría de Educación Pública, 2009). However, parents were still denied an input into administrative decisions. The change in the law seemed to strengthen the role of parent associations by allowing parents and/or their representatives to sit down and work with the head teachers, representatives of teachers and members of the community.

To that end, the law also expanded the role of the local, state and federal Asociación de Padres de Familia (APF) initially set up by Plutárco Elías Calles in 1929 as a counterweight to the then very conservative and clerical Union Nacional de Padres de Familia (UNPFO), which over the years came to play an important role in the government and the governing party. An apprenticeship in a leadership role in the APF was often a stepping stone in the political career of those who served in that capacity, and APF leaders played an important role in communicating official messages to parents and providing information about them to the governing bodies.

In general, these parent organizations had little influence on the educational system. What their members shared was an incredulity and even a bitterness that the reforms to open up the schools to parents were thwarted by the local, state and federal administrations, who put obstacles in their path that blocked them from even knowing what occurred within the schools themselves. Others pointed out that they were not provided with any secretarial backup and in many cases not even a desk was provided for their use. In some instances, they had little knowledge of the state system as they sent their children to private schools. Most had little contact with indigenous groups, particularly important in Yucatán where many primary schools use Maya as the language of instruction.

The role of parents: fictive and real

The results of these initiatives to expand parental participation prima facie have not lived up to expectation and, if anything, have confirmed to most parents that their input is always marginalized and sometimes even ignored. The CEPSs rarely function as they were intended. Although as individuals those parents who had the financial means and the time have always contributed to their schools and those without these resources have often provided support in kind and helped their children with their homework, as a group they are conspicuous by their absence from the life of most schools. This is particularly true in poor, rural and indigenous areas. In many urban areas parents are more visible at the school gates delivering or waiting for their children, with a few active parents running the school cooperatives and organizing school breakfasts.

The reasons for the failures of the CEPSs are many and varied. Politicians, policymakers and academics responsible for drawing up education reforms, anxious to find solutions, attribute the reluctance of parents to play a role in the education of their children to their passivity. The general view is that they are not fully able to understand how and what their children learn or should learn in the school. Moreover, they are unable to grasp the purpose and processes of assessment and school decision making. This echoes the long-standing view of politicians and policymakers that ordinary Mexicans are not yet educated enough to take on these responsibilities. Assigning responsibilities to them would lead to chaos. And only the party government can act in their best interests and eventually allow them to participate more fully in decision-making processes.

There are three general arguments in favour of the involvement of parents and the wider community in the day-to-day activities and running of schools and education systems. The first of these is that if parents and the wider community are actively involved in their children's education and in the management of the school more generally, educational performance improves (see also Martínez, 2009). To a large extent these improvements result from the school being able to draw upon a wider range of skills, time and effort that parents and the community can offer. The second is that given the importance of the school in equipping children with the requisite cultural capital and enhancing their life chances, parents and the community have the right to influence curricular and pedagogic practices in schools. The third is that in the Mexican case, wider participation can open up a closed system.

Traditionally, parental involvement is understood as a set of planned and deliberate individual actions, such as helping children with their homework and attending school-organized events. At the collective level, it was suggested that parents could be involved in their children's education by means of representation on policymaking committees and decision-making bodies at local authority or individual school levels (Alba, 2011). Parents are defined as the child's lawful guardians, and to some extent their family. Jones (2001, 19) argues that we should focus on the functional rather than the family connection between the child and the person who looks after them outside school; this is the notion of 'tutoring in support of children's achievement'.

Epstein's (2010) seminal work suggests three models of parental involvement: school-based participation, which consists of activities that are generally initiated by the school and take place there; home-based participation, which refers to activities normally initiated by the family and take place at home; and parent–teacher communication, which refers to exchanges of information between school and home with regards to students' progress and school programmes. This typology is based on the assumption that in order to substantially improve educational achievement, adopting joint practices between schools, families and communities is both feasible and desirable, given that their areas of influence overlap in children's learning and development. This view diverges from the idea that schools and families have separate roles and functions in relation to children's education.

Parental involvement in lower grades in general was found to be more significant in children's learning and contributed to lower dropout rates in high school (Barnard, 2004). Studies focusing on developing countries often report on parental contributions to school governance, particularly through decision making and finance, but studies from more affluent countries focus on their contribution to children's learning (see also Edge et al., 2008). In the area of school governance, parental involvement is found to be valuable in, for example, financial assistance for schools, often used to improve school infrastructure (see also Lugaz and De Grauwe, 2010). In the context of developing societies where schools lack basic facilities, this support is invaluable. This is often a popular form of parental assistance, but Lugaz and De Grauwe (2010) argue that it is a non-sustainable solution for school improvement and suggest parents should be given specific roles in relation to supervision and financial management, where this is feasible. Dearing et al. (2006) observed, in their longitudinal study, that increased parental attendance in meetings and events was linked to children's improved literacy. Domina (2005) however, has, argued that parents' voluntary work at school has more impact on a child's learning and behaviour than their involvement in trustee or parent–teacher associations, and this is supported by the claim that parents' attentions are diverted from their primary role of educating children if they are asked to help manage schools. Parental participation in children's learning can lead to increased motivation, concentration, attention and interest.

Factors relating to increasing parental involvement identified from the literature can be categorized into four areas (see also Edge et al., 2008): parents' motivational beliefs, perceptions of invitation and context that identify the approach and orientation of schools to parents, parents' own educational backgrounds and perceptions, and teachers' preparedness to collaborate with parents. In terms of motivational belief, parents were found to be motivated about their child's education when they believed that they had a role to play and the confidence and a sense of efficacy about their role, although those perceptions were conditioned by social contexts (Hoover-Dempsey et al., 2005).

In some countries parents are now less constrained by the barrier of the 'closed classroom door'. This occurs in different ways; for example, they may obtain detailed information about what happens at school via their networks with other parents, teachers and school administrators and, by doing so, they can customize their child's educational experience, especially through home-based interventions that mirror school activities. Likewise, some parents interact with their child's teachers to find out about academic opportunities so they can influence their child. In this regard, the degree of parents' social capital makes a difference. In addition to the advantages that some individual students have acquired from their parents' social capital, the quality, duration and intensity of the interaction between parents and schools increases these educational advantages. Nonetheless, the findings suggest that this form of proactive parental involvement tends to be concentrated in middle-class families (see also Hassrick and Schneider, 2009).

This form of parental involvement increases the degree of scrutiny of both teachers' practices and parents' private lives to the extent that other adults find out about what parents do at home with their children. Such a dynamic therefore may have both positive and negative implications; for example, teachers can develop a level of trust with parents, and parents and teachers are more likely to collaborate about developing learning programmes for their children. Parents can act together to support teachers in a timely and focused way when they are well informed about classroom activities. Thoughtful parental monitoring of classroom activities can increase teachers' responsiveness to their students' needs. On the negative side, parental surveillance may act to undermine teachers' professional judgement and practice. In addition, parents can exercise pressure to seek outside input on the selection of curricular programmes without consulting the school staff, increasing the vulnerability of teachers and school administrators and decreasing their effectiveness (Hassrick and Schneider, 2009).

Jeynes (2010) has drawn attention to the fact that the efficacy of a school's actions to foster parental involvement is likely to depend not so much on the specific guidelines and tutelage offered by schools to parents but on subtler elements (which have been overlooked in the past), such as the extent to which teachers, school principals and school staff in general are 'loving, encouraging, and supportive' to parents. One suggestion by Jeynes (2011) is that a parental involvement strategy instituted and maintained by the school is more important than parents teaching their child at home in isolation.

Parental involvement tends to decline during adolescence in marked contrast with the preschool stage, though a decline during students' adolescence is often mistakenly regarded by teachers and school administrators to be caused by a lack of willingness by parents to support their children at such a critical age, rather than an inability to work with schools in the interests of their child. Parents' participation in the school environment is limited by the fact that they commonly work long hours and have multiple responsibilities.

Six factors are found to be particularly unfavourable to parental participation: distrust of the education system, apathy, personal constraints and stress, inflexible schedules, transportation difficulties and teachers' dislike of different parenting styles (Jeynes, 2011). Edge et al. (2008) in their systematic review of the link between teacher quality and parental participation suggest that a primary determinant of parents' involvement in their children's education is the flexibility of their income generation; low-income families have significantly less time and flexibility to engage in such parenting activities. Interestingly, female parents who work part-time are found to be more involved than other parents in general, suggesting a link between maternal work and parental involvement. Berger and Riojas-Cortez (2015) make the point that for parental involvement and engagement to be effective, one of the many factors that need to be in place is the cooperation of employers so that parents can have real opportunities to become involved in the learning processes of their children.

Parental participation in Mexico

In a research project (Scott et al., 2012) we interviewed stakeholders in 11 states, working with local teams in primary and secondary schools in those states and then conducting in-depth research that drew upon the previous investigations in one municipality. Very little systematic research in Mexico has focused on this important area. In a reading of the literature we found only a small number of texts, such as Zurita et al. (2003) and Martínez et al. (2007). Rarely is the importance and role of the organizations representing parents discussed but, as we have seen, in most cases these organizations are themselves part of the power structure and their representatives are in that role as a means of advancing themselves politically. Santizo Rodall (2011), on the other hand, shows how significant changes are needed in school governance in order for parents to commit themselves to working in and with the school. This requires, she argues, a radical reforming of the top-down system, taking into account needs and aspirations so that poorer communities can see the value of a partnership and, we would add, so that the authorities can see that a radical change in attitudes and institutions is required if parents are to participate in the life of the school.

We start with the observation that terms like apathy, anomie, estrangement and a reluctance to participate, best summed up in Paulo Freire's culture of silence (1970), can be interpreted in various ways. Freire understood the silence he found among the poor and marginalized groups to be a survival strategy in the face of oppression rather than a willing submission. In a similar way, building on the work of Alexander Chayanov, George Foster (1965) coined the term 'limited good' to characterize the peasants' sense of injustice if their basic needs (the limited good) were not met. Even more to the point is James C. Scott's (1985) notion of 'passive resistance' or 'informal resistance' where the disadvantaged opt for forms of indirect dissent and resistance, such as foot-dragging or dissimulation, that end up being far more effective and less risky than outright protest. This is a form of participation reticence.

What we found puzzling when we first sat down with parents to try to learn why they did not participate more fully in school life was that they just did not have the time due to their multiple commitments at home and at work, indicating a strong insulation between home and school. Taken at face value this might seem to be the end of the story. But as we will try to show, behind a simple statement are implicit meanings or notions that may seem obvious to the respondent, but are hidden from the enquirer.

Parental participation reticence was faithfully recorded in Zurita et al. (2003), in Martinez et al. (2007) and in a work on citizen's civic participation in the political process more generally (see also Aguayo, 2008). All these studies suggest that the culprit is apathy, the apathy of the population to assume responsibility for public affairs. Some attribute this to the systemic clientelism that we discussed earlier. In a separate research project conducted at school-zone level in central Jalisco (see also Martin and Guzman, 2016), we found that with over half of the population living and working outside the municipality, mainly in the United States, the time of most heads of households was consumed by income-generating activities and the burden of domestic work. However, it emerged that their attitudes to schooling were also governed by other factors that led us towards a fuller understanding of parental participation reticence.

A parent's representative argued that, '(p)arents are not used to participating in education; they tend to leave it to the teachers', and this was typical of what school representatives of the Asociación de Padres de Familia (APF) and individual parents reported. Never having been consulted, they simply had no experience of being asked their opinions. They were suspicious as to why they were suddenly being solicited to give their views to those who, even if they were not authorities, had the authorities' permission to interview them. We realized that we had to probe more deeply.

Sergio Aguayo (2010) has attributed the co-opted character of public life in Mexico to the social apathy citizens display towards government institutions. In schools, the absence of a two-way relationship between teachers and parents is an example of Aguayo's apathy. Bracho and Zamudio (1997) document the failure of Mexican parent–teacher organizations in these terms, arguing that they are not effective because parents are unaccustomed to voicing their opinions and intervening in matters that directly concern their children's educational progress and welfare. Parents do participate in specific activities, like preparing and serving school breakfasts, cleaning classrooms and financial contributions. They are also obliged to show up for official meetings. But here as elsewhere, their involvement is on the terms set by the school and there is no attempt to establish a more egalitarian and participative partnership. When parents want to express dissent or opinions contrary to those of the teachers they have to accept that this may run the risk of reprisals against their children. From the teachers' perspective, parental intervention is seen as complicating their already overburdened day and potentially creating problems with the education authorities. The result is a 'divorce of convenience' whereby each side of the relationship seeks to avoid all but the most minimal contact with the other.

The 1992 agreement (Acuerdo Nacional para la Modernización de la Educación Basica (ANMEB)) proposed a new relationship between the administration, the teachers and users of the educational system, and, through subsequent official agreements, between the key partners in state education. However, the government responded only at a surface level to the real involvement of service users, potential users and the wider society. Participation has been restricted to top-level academic consultative forums and the endorsement of school programmes by officially created organizations such as parents' associations. Policies such as more extensive involvement of parents in the education of their children are compromised in the Mexican context by the contingencies and constraints of the institutional setting. This includes not just parents in the school setting but also importantly, the teachers' union (SNTE). Once the trade union was satisfied that social participation would not affect salaries and conditions of service, the government embarked on a double-pronged strategy composed of decentralizing still more powers to the 32 state governments and finding a way of incorporating sometimes disaffected parents into the system.

The 1993 law which followed the ANMEB, whilst gesturing towards devolving powers to more local levels, control of the curriculum, pedagogy, the school calendar, assessment, evaluation and the provision of financial resources were reserved for the federal government alone. The local state authorities existed primarily to oversee those functions without having any role in their determination. In other words, parents' participation remained limited within prescribed official limits. Their independent voice would still not be heard.

The federal government obliged state and municipal authorities to set up such associations, which in addition to having the same duties as individual parents were obliged to inform the state and federal authorities of any difficulties they encountered. They thus served as conduits to report discontent in the schools but were not provided with resources to solve any problems related to this discontent. Although the government made provision for courses for parents, these rarely took place.

At the same time, there was little encouragement for parents to work with teachers. The key person in these new associations was the president who, depending upon where he or she was located, could be actively involved or merely a factotum. Being a president of a parental organization was a step up the political ladder and needed political connections to be chosen and supported, as was clearly explained to us by the presidents of the associations of Colima and Tabasco and was evident in the case of the current national President of the Parents' Association who came from Nayarit. Some other presidents were hard-working, such as the presidents in Aguascalientes, Jalisco and Sinaloa. Some demonstrated how little power even a president had in order to have an effect on the educational progress of their own children. On the whole, parent organizations had little input into the educational system unless their leaders were educators themselves, as is the case in Yucatán. Even then, they had limited influence and often used the office as a way to achieve political advancement. Their knowledge of education varied greatly, with the Jalisco and Sinaloa presidents being very well informed and the Coahuila and Tabasco presidents having very little to say except to promote the need for a disciplined workforce. A theme shared by all 11 presidents we interviewed was the need to encourage greater parental participation in education and address child abuse, which according to some is widespread in the schools.

The federal and state educational authorities continue to be dominant in school administration, something that Justa Ezpeleta suggested as long ago as 1990 and has reiterated more recently (2004). Even the limited areas in which the CEPSs are allowed to operate have been circumscribed. Officially they should have just over half of the representation on the council by occupying the presidency. Yet because this has not barred the head teacher from assuming the presidency, it has become the norm in the schools of the municipality studied here. A notable exception is the special case of Colima where the Education Secretariat has barred head teachers from holding this position (see also Santizo Rodall, 2010).

State representatives of the Asociación de Padres de Familia (APF) revealed a mixed picture of the impact that their organizations had on the school. The majority reported that they had an uphill struggle to make their voices heard, largely because they were excluded from all matters dealing with the curriculum and how it was taught. The main concern of the authorities was to enlist their support for school improvements and to cover running costs not provided by state and federal authorities. One respondent argued that although she had developed a good working relationship with the authorities, parents were nevertheless loath to make their opinions heard about the running of their schools: '(t)hey need to be encouraged and taught to do so because they are not accustomed to doing so'.

The majority of the APF representatives interviewed were concerned with problems of discipline and, in particular, with child abuse and other forms of teacher misconduct. Whilst lamenting the lack of initiative of the parents to break through the traditional hold teachers and officials had on school life they were unable to suggest how this could be achieved. As is often the case, mass surveys in Mexico display strong support for teachers and the institutions of public education (see Basañez, 1990, and Flores Andrade, 2014). We found the same in our survey of the municipality of Buenavista, central Jalisco. We also found that only 2 per cent of the interviewees knew anything at all about the purpose of CEPSs. They said that they had never been informed about these new institutions, even though only a few months earlier, in the Spring of 2010, schools had received the instructions they needed to activate these representative organizations. Our negative findings and conclusions are similar to those of the more probing micro studies and ethnographic research investigations that forensically examine these general opinions and reveal deep disquiet about the quality of education in the country (see also Martin, 2007). Consequently, whilst very few parents ranked the quality of education highly, the majority nonetheless thought it was 'just about satisfactory', despite a concern with teachers' high-handedness and absenteeism and the fact that too many secondary school graduates failed to go on to higher education. The majority of respondents who attended CEPS meetings maintained that the organization was restricted to dealing with mundane matters such as organizing school breakfasts, cleaning and rubber-stamping head teacher applications for SEP national programmes.

Discrimination and playing the system

Parents are marginalized and subsequently discriminated against in three ways. The first tactic is that a teacher or head teacher simply ignores the rules, usually because they consider themselves immune from sanctions or because no one is really assessing their compliance with these rules. A good example of this is a teacher expelling a pupil without giving a reason and in contradiction to the rules that only permit exclusions when the child is a real danger to other children. A second tactic is when the official interprets the rules and simulates a procedure, normally to avoid a time-consuming activity, one that complicates their life, or because the official receives some personal benefit from this rule bending, for example, in acting as a gatekeeper for some resource or benefit. Tactic three is a variant of this. This occurs when an over-strict application of a regulation, or the invention of one, is used in dealing with parents. An example is denying a transfer for reasons of strict transparency, or being bureaucratically evasive when they submit a complaint to the authorities. This is well summed up by Benito Juárez's famous dictum, 'Justice for my friends; the law for my enemies'. We found examples of each of these three tactics. According to our key informants in the schools that we studied closely, teachers' meetings devoted to the establishment of the CEPSs were focused on rule bending, evasive and simulation tactics (i.e. tactics one and two) and devising strategies to exclude parents from participating in decision making.

The rules governing the forming of the councils stipulate that there must be a parental majority of 50 per cent +1. But this is undermined, as we have seen, if associates and/or friends of the head teachers are co-opted, if parent members are also teachers in the school or another local school, or if the head teacher assumes the presidency, which was usually the case. The rules of the councils are such that parents have no role in the hiring and firing of teachers or in curriculum and pedagogic matters. However, where a matter arises involving possible teacher misconduct or their incompetency and this is deemed to directly affect the children's progress and well-being in school, parents may become involved. Furthermore, in some schools, parents have actually been invited to participate in some areas of teaching (see, for example, Chapter 6).

In the school zone we observed and the vast majority of other state educational authorities where we conducted research, parents were excluded completely from any activities involving teaching, the curriculum, pedagogy and policy development. Here a mix of tactics one and two is the rule, that is, a restrictive reading of the rules, and keeping parents uninformed about them and their right to participate. In practice in Buenavista, their role continued to be confined to: attending meetings called by their children's class teacher or to collect school reports; responding to particular matters concerning their children's performance or behaviour; making payments for school upkeep; the organization of school breakfasts; and attending school open days, feast days and events to mark public holidays. A parent described the situation in the following way: '(t)he teacher only wants to see me when there is a problem'; and 'when they need some money', added her companion. In the focus groups on parental participation, we saw that parents had not been informed about their role in the newly activated CEPSs. In one of the schools, the first time that the parents had heard of these new organizations was in a meeting when a senior training official addressed the parents. Following this meeting one parent said that:

> It is difficult to participate as we should because we do not know how. We have only just learned about these CEPSs. I knew about the Safety and Emergency committees, but not the CEPSs. I did not know they were all part of the same thing. We have not been informed.

Parents emphatically resented being kept in the dark about matters that directly concerned them. Then to make matters worse, they were made party to their own exclusion from school participation. One way that the head teacher and his staff circumvented the official requirement to set up the CEPS is to engage in an exercise in simulation (i.e. tactic one). A parent who attended the meeting to establish the CEPS in one of the primary schools explained it in this way:

> They asked us to come to the parents meeting and then asked us for volunteers to make up the school council, but then, once having the names, they would not have to bother us again! I mean that does not sound as if they want us to take part in anything or for us to have a voice, does it?

Two teachers and a parent reported on a similar incident early on in the school year 2011–12. One of the teachers explained it in the following way:

> The head teacher called us for the first parents meeting of the school year. About half of the parents were there. We were told that we needed to form a council. He said we did not need to worry too much about obligations. All he needed was a few names to send to the authorities and that would be that. Of course, put that way, no one wanted to volunteer – just to rubber-stamp the head's paperwork. X's brother was asked and he refused outright to be associated with such a pretence.

All the teachers thought it important to be able to count on parental support for the education of their children and to lend a hand with practical tasks in the school. However, it was rare to hear teachers favouring a regular partnership with parents.

Previously, we argued that official top-down administrative procedures of local, state and federal authorities hindered parental participation. Within the schools themselves the attitudes and actions of the teachers added another layer of obstacles, 'discretionary practices' or what in reality was defensive obstructionism. Although parents generally did not make explicit that this might be a reason why they participated so little in the life of the school, one parent argued that: '(t)hey don't take any notice of our comments so there is no point in participating. They don't listen'.

Head teachers and teachers invest a great deal of effort and energy in trying to exclude parents. Teachers were worried about increasing demands on their already overcrowded timetables. In addition, loyalty to the trade union was their only real protection against the authorities and they were willing to forgo possible alliances with parents because the trade union did not favour them. Union regulations are an inescapable part of a teacher's working conditions. As the SNTE representative of one of the schools said when questioned on the issue of complaints against teachers: '(m)y primary responsibility is to defend any teacher accused of malpractice'. The union's defence of its members considerably outweighed anything that an individual parent, with limited time and funds, might be able to do.

The bureaucratic discretion that the teachers engage in is in part to prevent parents getting too close to the teachers' professional domain, but it is also a way of dealing with the flood of directives issuing from the SEP authorities whose many departments make no effort to coordinate and regulate the flow of their directives. The authorities also fail to follow up, monitor and evaluate the impact of their directives (see also Alba, 2011). Neither have attempts been made to identify obstacles to their fulfilment, such as a lack of teacher preparation, poor timing and institutional problems that hinder the activation of the CEPSs. Such schools have made what efforts they can to carry out official instructions under the normal conditions of excess demands and insufficient support and supervision. This most commonly results in the use of various discretionary tactics, especially (according to the frequency the term cropped up in our interviews) bureaucratic pretence or simulation and the consequent failure to encourage parental participation, so traditionally absent from Mexican school life.

Two mothers, objecting to the way schools only solicit parental participation when they need money, spoke of teachers as such:

> Mother 1: They demand money shamelessly, not considering that we are hard up, but they are fine, thank you very much. They may not earn much but they have a job for life.
> Mother 2: It's just not right, the teachers, with their admittedly small, but at least secure salaries, waste so much time in class when we who are hard up, depend on our children getting a decent education to make their way in the world.

Another parent said:

> It is difficult for us to help with our children's learning because, for example in my case, I really do not feel competent to help them. I have some schooling but not enough to do much for my children.

Some respondents maintained that their main concern was to obtain a greater role for parents and the need to compel the teachers to work with them; however, the system regarded parents as an annoyance rather than an asset and ally for educational improvement. They were irritated that they were not provided with the help, facilities and materials they required to allow the new curriculum with its emphasis on child-based learning to function effectively.

So far, we have concentrated on how the educational services thwart parental participation. However, as we have suggested, the parents express guilt at not doing more to support the school, the teachers and their own children. During group and individual meetings that we arranged we asked parents why they were not more active in these respects. The immediate reply, as we have seen, was that they just did not have the time because of their many commitments at home and in their work. In these sessions self-reproach was not translated into a willingness to be more involved in anything other than an ancillary activity such as organizing school breakfasts. That is, no one envisaged parents dealing with the areas of curriculum, pedagogy and administration (see also Martínez et al., 2007). Why is there such a gulf between contrition and action?

The claim of having heavy workloads and little time is aligned with what is known about this and many other migrant towns in Mexico and about poor rural and indigenous communities. In the specific case of a typical migrant town, more than half of Buenavista is living and working elsewhere (Ortiz Gonzàlez, 1998). Whilst this has permitted an inflow of remittances to sustain the family, and even to support public works and other charitable activities on a modest scale, it also lays a heavy burden on those who remain, predominantly women, the old and children.

Moreover, families in such communities not receiving remittances often have to find work, always badly paid, locally. Many women, in particular, spend large amounts of time working in the fields, as domestic servants or street sellers when their children are at school. Older siblings or grandparents often look after the younger children. Older children have to combine schooling with work. Grandparents and other older members of the family may be able to care for children for short periods of time but they too often have to work, and failing health and other commitments can curtail their child support. Religious obligations can use up as much as five hours a week of family time with its services, catechisms and feasts. To be eligible for the small amount of help that social services provide, when available, a quarter to one-third of Buenavista families were subject to lengthy administrative procedures that also entailed workfare obligations.

According to one of the local educational psychologists, the parents clearly feel guilty about this:

> Nowadays in Buenavista, and elsewhere, parents are frowned upon if they punish their children too severely. In one sense this is good, to do away with cruelty, but the downside is that although the children now have rights, they do not have obligations. Parents don't put limits on them. They have lost authority. In addition, mothers who traditionally take most responsibility for their children, now go out to work, because what the husband earns is insufficient. Hence, the mothers harbour a sense of guilt towards the children for giving them insufficient attention, so they spoil them.

That is, in rural Mexico there are many forces that work against parental support for schooling. The most important of these is the fragmentation of the family as a result of economic insecurity, labour migration, the social division of labour in poor and indigenous communities and the advent of the narcotics economy. Parents tend to avoid confrontations with teachers and demanding funds, in-kind contributions and organizational support in the running of the school, and even sharing the teachers' teaching load through homework, all under the Damocles sword of potential reprisals against their children. They evade these demands, even if this means neglecting what they consider to be their responsibilities towards their children.

Christopher Lasch spoke of a similar phenomenon in a different context, and the contrast with Buenavista is instructive. In *The Culture of Narcissism* (1979), he analysed what he saw as a growing trend among the middle class in mainly urban USA. He drew upon authors of the social history of childhood who have studied the long-term trend that places childhood at the centre of social life. He suggested that the contemporary sanctification of childhood was a late twentieth-century economic trend. The terms of trade for educated women between (increasingly automated) household tasks and salaried labour have increasingly favoured middle-class women replacing their own domestic labour with hired help and developing their careers, supported by the feminist movement.

In the United States, it is middle-class upward mobility that drives the recent trend in childhood neglect/overprotection; in rural Mexico, it is something more fundamental. This is the fragmentation of the family as a result of economic insecurity and labour outmigration. Parents evade school demands, and are torn between their income-generating activities and the realization that they need to support their children. Given the immediately pressing exigencies of the household, they end up turning their back on the school, that in the circumstances seems partly justified both by their workloads and their annoyance towards the school.

This therefore leads to a 'divorce of convenience'. The two parties, parents and teachers, fail to reach an agreement. Each sees the error in the other's behaviour. Conciliation proves impossible because there are no conciliators or arbitrators in Mexican education. Instead the authorities, the administration and the teachers' union, set the rules for all aspects of schooling, including parental participation. The weaker party, the parents, resent this but realize they can do little, so, with a deep sense of failing in their responsibility for their children, they withdraw from the school. Like all divorces, the children are the ones that suffer from this broken relationship. A potentially productive, fertile marriage is turned into the educational equivalent of a broken home.

The institutional and educational leviathan that is education in Mexico lacks any independent channels for parents to express and resolve their concerns satisfactorily (Aguayo, 2010). In the end it is based upon the premise that those channels that exist are there exclusively to inform and at times instruct parents in what they should do. We have seen that the national educational authorities are beyond the critical reach of most parents and within the school, teachers have developed a whole range of strategies to keep parents at arm's length.

They include the inflexible and often arbitrary imposition of rules and regulations that protect teachers from having to deal with everyday parents' concerns. Having already found themselves constrained by unmanageable and often unworkable teaching loads, along with bureaucratic demands, time-consuming and questionable evaluations, not to mention the Kafka-like procedures they have to fulfil to sustain their service conditions, they fall back on an arsenal of evasion techniques.

What we have called participation reticence and others have called passive resistance is the fruit of dysfunctional educational arrangements that work against parental participation in the school. How can one transform this vicious circle into a virtuous one? In our research, we only saw one example of successful parental intervention where parents acted together against an abusive teacher. Elsewhere in Mexico, one finds some isolated examples of sustained parental participation, as we will see in the next chapter. Silence and a reluctance to participate is not simply a result of parents' apathy or disinterest but also originates in the circumstances and conditions described above. In the next chapter, we examine intercultural education practices and alternative education programmes.

6
Intercultural Education and Alternative Education Programmes

Over the past two and a half decades in Mexico we have witnessed a spectacular growth of voluntary and community organizations, including self-help groups, cooperatives and social enterprise movements, usually conceived of and operating independently of the government. They belong neither to the public nor the private sector. They are generally called third sector Organizations (TSOs) and have come to play a significant role with regards to rural and small-scale development and in establishing education programmes in places that government institutions barely reach. Many have developed alternative educational practices designed to be more relevant to the needs of the communities in which they operate. The work of educational professionals from within the state education institutions is less well known.

Although there is a growing literature on the rise of third sector organizations in an increasingly vocal and sometimes disorganized civil society, the story of third sector organizations undertaking root-and-branch transformation of public education from the inside has not been told. This chapter begins this task and asks the question: Can they play an important role in overcoming the obstacles we have discussed in previous chapters to reforming education in Mexico? Drawing on field research and over 20 years' knowledge and experience of these organizations, we will attempt to show that the education they promote and, in some cases, practise is more in line with public opinion about what education should be in Mexico than that of official bodies. Although they are small in number and most operate in the micro-settings of the schools and school catchment areas, they are the most active educators in the country, combining cutting-edge pedagogy with attention to the most educationally neglected populations.

A second aspect of these educational third sector organizations presents us with a curious paradox: although they are often staffed by officially registered educational personnel – and are active in the state educational system – as a result of their activities, they find themselves marginalized or in conflict with that very system, even whilst insisting that they are untiring defenders of state education. In other words, the third sector organizations find themselves *in* the system, but not *of* it.

The third feature concerns the third sector organizations' critiques of official education that are directed not only against the authorities but also against the official trade union (the SNTE) that claims to represent the interests of education workers. The third sector organizations draw their inspiration from two main sources. The first is fulfilling the needs and demands of the learning community they aspire to serve (a term first used by Jean Lave and Étienne Wenger in 1991), namely, the students, their parents and their community. These constituencies consist of marginalized rural indigenous peasants and workers, deskilled teachers working in the state sector, the disaffected middle class that continues to send its children to state schools and even elements of the entrepreneurial sector, angry at what they see as Mexico's increasing uncompetitiveness. The second source of inspiration comes from national and international currents of progressive thought and action in education and social change. Typically, it is the often middle-class organic intellectual leadership of these third sector organizations that provides the impetus through their networking. These contacts within the educational and cognate sectors, and with wider currents of thought and action, help compensate for the support they are denied from the official educational system. This strength in collaboration and in connectedness with the wider world contrasts with and circumvents the closed, hierarchical clientelistic networks of the official administration.

The independent efforts of these organizations are considered to be necessary as a result of a fourth characteristic: the conviction that the officially stipulated schedules and provision of time, and indeed space, for those working in education is insufficient to achieve even some of the most basic tasks. As such, the third sector organizations consider that they must add time and effort to what is the norm. This gives rise to a large amount of volunteering, regardless of whether there are other resource and funding bases for their work.

One measure of the success of these organizations would be to gauge how much impact they have had on policy and to what extent their models of operation have been applied. Most of the third sector organizations studied did not seek to influence the general educational policy agenda. Indeed, they have tended to distrust such activity. The principal claim of most of the organizations studied is that the official system is failing to do what its policies are designed and/or claim to do. Also, they have committed themselves to teaching the curriculum, using an up-to-date relevant pedagogy and encouraging dedicated teachers to work hand in hand with parents. This means that these third sector organizations focus less on policy as such, much of which they agree with, and more on the autocratic and clientelistic behaviour of the administration responsible for implementing it. Their critiques and work are important for the practice of building learning communities and providing more effective teaching and learning programmes.

Third sector organizations in Mexico

The Mexican third sector organizations in the field of education include private charities, business-related organizations and religious organizations of various denominations. Their activities vary from establishing their own independent schools to devising programmes for such groups as the young, rural producers and women to provide professional and entrepreneurial skills. Funding comes from the private sector, national and international programmes of education and cultural organizations, such as the 'Escuelas de Calidad', a direct initiative of the SEP, or reading programmes sponsored by the Consejo Nacional para la Cultura y las Artes (Conaculta).

Educational third sector organizations can be broadly classified into six types. The first of these is indigenous-based popular organizations led mainly by teachers in rural areas. These are organizations like the Congreso Nacional de Educación Indígena e Intercultural (CNEII), Educación Comunitaria Indígena para el Desarrollo Autónomo (ECIDEA) and the Tatutsi Maxakwaxi programme. The second type is independent teacher-based organizations in various parts of the country, particularly in marginal, rural and poor urban areas, notably *Tamachtini*, the Movimiento de Innovación y Transformación de la Educación Básica (MITEB), Centro Educativo Narciso Bassols (CENB), Bases Magisteriales, Innovación Educativa (INED) and Contracorriente. The third type is broadly based citizens' associations of all political colours opposed to what they see as trade-union and SEP incompetence and abuse of power. Academic groups like Observatorio Ciudadano de Educación (OCE) fall into this category, as do the Asociación Civil Hacia una Cultura Democrática (ACUDE), the Incidencia Civica en Educación (ICE) and Mexicanos Primero.

The fourth type is university extension programmes that provide pedagogic resources and organizational and developmental support for local educational centres in poor areas. The Instituto Tecnológico y de Estudios Superiores de Occidente (ITESO) is an example. The fifth type is business charities like those related to two of the major banks: Bancomer and Banamex (when it was controlled by Alfredo Harp Helú and his family) and the Laboratorios Julio. Finally, there are religious organizations that usually create or directly support educational projects. These include schools supported by Comunidades de Base influenced by liberation theology, like Fomento Educativo y Cultural (CEREAL) and private schools and institutions under the aegis of Opus Dei. To varying degrees all but the business charities work within educational institutions with the support of students and their families.

As we have seen, the highly centralized educational system presided over a rapid expansion of education from the 1940s onwards but sacrificed quality through economies of scale, such as a shorter school day, permitting double-shift teaching and such devices as multigrade teaching and distance learning and reduced spending on teachers. From the late 1970s, specialist researchers, officials and the media increasingly voiced concern with high dropout rates and poor educational quality more generally. As a response, the Mexican government began to undertake administrative reforms leading up to relocating some operational functions from the federal government to the states. But this occurred during an era of economic liberalization marked by budget cuts in the public sector. These policies did not lead to any improvement in educational performance. In fact, by the time the various international league tables began appearing in the late 1990s, Mexico's poor educational performance had become indisputably a matter of public concern.

The two PAN governments that were in office from 2000–12 opted for, respectively, teacher professional development via payment by results (the Carrera Magisterial) and standardized aptitude testing (SATs) as strategies for lifting Mexico out of the educational doldrums. The former was soon undermined by cronyism and by poorly designed cascade refresher courses. SATs were being introduced in Mexico as a means of upgrading educational quality at the time when in some parts of the world this type of approach was becoming discredited. High impact testing sits uncomfortably with the newly reformed curriculum, which emphasizes creativity and child-centred learning, and this has led to teaching to the test and thus to a distortion of the curriculum.

Making test-driven teacher and student evaluation the cornerstone of educational policy in recent years rather than improving student performance only served to show up the continued inequalities in provision. An OECD report (2013) on Mexico indicated that current courses intended to upgrade the teaching professional were counterproductive. A recent World Economic Forum report (2016–17) on educational performance places Mexico 102nd in a list of 124 countries and in the 2015 PISA report, Mexico was at the bottom of the OECD country tables, a position it has occupied for the last 15 years.

We have seen that Mexico's state education, tightly controlled and insular as it is, has brooked little intervention from within the system or from outside Mexico. Research conducted more than 10 years after the Education Act of 1993 that legislated for parental and community participation in schools confirmed that the legislation has not been fully enacted (see also Basave, 2010). Paradoxically, the Mexican authorities are highly sensitive to international opinion, especially to their evaluations of Mexico's performance in international league tables. Nevertheless, they resist what they consider inappropriate interventions by 'externals'. Moreover, the break in decades of PRI rule that occurred in 2000 did not significantly change institutional practices. Educational issues remained of less importance than the political issues of control over resources and processes (see also Basave, 2010).

The emergence of independent dissent

Discontent with bureaucratic closed-shop cronyism from independent associations emanated from the broad-based anti-government demonstrations of the 1968 and 1971 protests, the guerrilla movements in the countryside in the 1970s, the post-1985 earthquake local citizens support movement and teacher-union protests at the end of the 1960s, 1970s and 1980s. The 1980s were years of structural adjustment, austerity and public-sector cuts, resulting in 'la crisis', which according to some sources put nearly 50 per cent of the population on or below the poverty line (Instituto Nacional de Estadística y Geografía, 2013). In 1986 salaries were reduced to their lowest point in decades. Dissatisfaction with the existing regime was manifest in the formation of the Frente Democrático that nearly, and, according to many, actually toppled the PRI in the 1988 presidential elections.

The Salinas government of 1988–94 had extended economic liberalization, but at the same time opened the way for the construction of new partnerships between government and people through the welfare programme, 'Solidaridad'. This approach devolved some services and social support to more local levels, encouraging citizens' participation in development in official programmes and independent non-governmental organizations (NGOs). Successful applications from poor and neglected areas seeking NGO status and funds were restricted by policies of fiscal austerity, brought about by the previous PRI administration. Thus, far from seeing themselves as partners with the government, many were its antagonists. There was a clear movement away from support for the poor. Verduzco and Tapia's research (2012) shows that although 30 per cent of funds were given to TSOs working in poverty alleviation, only 6 per cent of the funds went to the non-governmental organizations.

The impact of pauperization and marginalization, combined with rising expectations encouraged by the government, and the failure to contain the discontent it generated was reflected in the educational sector. The protests of the Coordinadora Nacional de Trabajadores de la Educación (CNTE), active from 1980 onwards, have been the most widespread protest against both the administration and the SNTE for their perceived cronyism and authoritarianism. According to other dissident groups like the Educación y Cambio group that published Cero de Conducta, the CNTE later succumbed just as much to cronyism as did the organizations it was criticizing.

Other educational third sector organizations appeared in the 1990s. Among these were the Bases Magisteriales, MITEB, CENB and Maravatío (see also Street, 2001). The Zapatista uprising of 1994 was perhaps the clearest indication of popular disaffection with established rule in Mexico. This movement has had a long-term impact on independent social activism as well as catalysing movements to reclaim indigenous identities. It sought to redress the official neglect of or even hostility to indigenous mother tongues and the culture and knowledge of the pre-Hispanic peoples of Mexico.

The social currents of alienation from the PRI regime were not limited to the left and to the popular classes. From the mid 1990s, dissatisfaction with the one-party rule of the PRI led to the expansion of the hitherto small centre-right National Action Party (PAN). As with the left, the centre and right of the political spectrum consisted not just of the new parties (notably the left Frente Democrático) but also the smaller associations and groups. In the educational sphere, there was a growing number of private schools for the disaffected middle class. At university level, the hegemony of the UNAM as the source of political leaders began to give way to the establishment of private institutions, notably the Instituto Tecnologico Autonomo de Mexico (ITAM) and the Instituto Tecnologico y d Estudios Superiores de Monterrey (ITESM). A glance at the register of NGOs over the past 20 years gives some indication of the diversity of these independent organizations. These groups worked at local, regional and national levels and raised an increasing range of issues, most importantly that education should not be considered to be the exclusive province of the government.

The current list of registered third sector organizations working in education shows that the majority are church-based and business-related organizations. Among the most well known are the Monte de Piedad and the Charities of Carlos Slim. Typically, this, the largest sector, established their own educational institutions or provided supplements to mainstream public education, such as books, educational materials and equipment, computers and even buildings. Exceptionally, the Laboratorios Julio collaborated with the SNTE, setting up conferences and joint one-off projects. The Fundación Empresarios por la Educación Básica has been involved in the area of school management.

The other main area in which third sector organizations work is policy. The most active of these organizations is Mexicanos Primero that now has more than 100 affiliates. Mexicanos Primero is a pressure group, or watchdog, claiming to represent the interests of the citizen in public education. A notable exception to this religious inclination is OCE, founded in 1998, which has acted as a commentator on educational policy via regular publication in the mass media (see also Sutton and Levinson, 2001).

Beyond the revolution

Manuel Castells (1996) suggests that rather than wait for the revolution heralding the collapse of capitalism, social movements are usually established prior to this. They promote an alternative lifestyle, turning their backs on mainstream society and establishing their own post-revolutionary organizations consisting of cooperatives, shared housing, alternative economic strategies and so on. Mexico has followed this path, starting with the 1985 post-earthquake citizens' activism and then just over eight years later, the Zapatista uprising. Many of the educational third sector organizations are also part of broader social movements arguing for grass-roots social change. Tatutsi and Tatei projects, for example, go beyond,

> the mere collection of educational information, but rather press into service this information in order to help improve the learning taking place and construct an educational and social project for the community (See Tertulia IV, DF., 2012.)

The most outspoken groups leaving the existing system behind can be found in the indigenous third sector organizations. In the second National Conference of the CNEII, in Oaxaca in 2010, the steering committee emphasized its determination to create a new educational agenda for the indigenous people of Mexico:

> One of our fundamental strategies has been to exchange experiences of indigenous education at field level, in the places that they are being developed, and discuss these activities in the schools among the organisations carrying them out, their curricula, their pedagogy. We have been in the Mixteca, Chihuahua, Yucatan, Michoacan with the Purepecha, in the Sierra Huichola and in Chiapas and other places . . . We have been organising training programmes to develop . . . proposals for advancing indigenous education, focusing, among other things, on indigenous languages, including the methodology of language nests (see below). (Introductory address of the anti-discrimination conference of the CNEII in Oaxaca, 12 June 2010.)

The CNEII has been strongly committed to a 'from-the-base-up' methodology, as well as developing educational schemes focused on the experience of local educators and learning from experienced local and national educators together with indigenous educators from other parts of the world. Even the methodology of the CNEII conferences and the consultative and consensual decision making were different from official institutions. The same applies to other indigenous education associations, notably Tatutsi, ECIDEA and the Coalicion de Maestros y Promotores Indigenas de Oaxaca (CMPIO)-supported projects. In terms of actual learning centres, the Secundarias Comunitarias not only set up state schools where none existed previously but also established unique curricula, and materials produced on site, underpinned by local knowledge, language and culture. Similarly, in other regions, where public education had not previously been available, innovative educational programmes centred on local cultures, notably Tatutsi in the Huichol highlands and initiatives in many Purépecha-speaking areas of Michoacan.

The breadth and depth of their work and the way they conduct it go far beyond the official ethos. Projects range from mobile laboratories in remote areas; on-site teacher upgrading; arts and music outreach programmes; school community development projects; the production of indigenous language texts together with instruction in their use; and 'learning nests' in the indigenous mother tongue in homes.

Yet rather than advertise the uniqueness of their work, their attention is focused on the next challenge or how to obtain the resources needed to accomplish it. Visiting these projects is like visiting researchers in their laboratories: the focus is on their work, the problems they encounter and how they intend to solve them. This seems to the activists the most sensible, even the only, way of working, although it contrasts sharply with the way most of their colleagues in the official system work, and indeed how they themselves worked beforehand. The new way appears to them to be the most natural thing to do. In this sense, one can say that they are living in the post-transformation world, to use Castells' (1996) phrase.

Sidestepping the state: finding space between the cracks

Independent educators have come up with an alternative stratagem that we will call sidestepping the state authorities. One teacher of Signos, the independent school that has outreach bolt-on reading programmes in different parts of Mexico, described this strategy as: 'finding the cracks in the SEP structure and knowing how to take advantage of them'. James Scott dealt with this phenomenon when examining the very different context of pre-capitalist Southeast Asia. He argued that the reason why some societies have not evolved into centralized states is not because of technological or cultural backwardness, but as the result of a deliberate decision and a disinclination to concentrate power in one source (Scott, 2010). The members of these smaller societies simply turn away from such developments and from neighbouring societies seeking to incorporate them into their own way of working. This avoidance or sidestepping an apparently irreversible or powerful force is what these third sector organizations do in relation to the apparently all-powerful education authorities.

These third sector organizations sidestep the authorities by disappearing under their radar or beyond their normal reach. They find it necessary to resort to such stratagems in order to teach. The SEP is wary of any sign of autonomy, even when this is simply to enable teachers to carry out stated official policy. Their priority is obedience to the authorities and conformity with the unwritten codes of behaviour among educational personnel. Educational imperatives come second and are always motivated by political imperatives. However, the third sector organizations that have managed to operate for any length of time, have without exception relied on their personal connections in the SEP. Just as an inspector can ignore policy in order to reward or punish his or her teachers, so a friend of a senior official may waive hierarchical protocols to allow their friend to develop educational innovations with their team, especially if they can in return share the credit for success with senior officials or patrons.

Hence, these organizations need leaders with links to patrons/senior personnel who are willing and able to support their projects. This support at a minimum level takes the form of deflecting undue scrutiny, interference and sanctions. On occasions patrons may take a special interest in alternative projects for various reasons besides friendship. MITEB was favoured by strong political companionship with personnel in the left-of-centre Zacatecas state government of the 2000s. The newly created quasi-governmental authority, Coordination of Indigenous and Intercultural Education, proved an ally during the same period to the recently formed CNEII, connecting it with sources of finance and involving it in events and consultations at the time when the government needed to generate working relationships with the indigenous communities.

Religious or ex-religious activists benefit from wide networks and influence in many government circles and in civil society. One former Salesian was a founder of the *Tamachtini* TV secondary schools (*telesecundarias*) that evolved into a national programme. He became a school inspector in a rural area of the state of Puebla and his influence in official circles enabled him to develop a more innovative, community-linked version of TV secondary schools than that provided by the poorly functioning national programme. Another closely related TV secondary school network in the same state relied on a committed senior inspector working with Contracorriente. Other projects take advantage of their geographical remoteness, making it difficult for officials to monitor the schools involved even though they are official schools.

The need for such elaborate subterfuges illustrates the extent to which the SEP and its associated organizations are top-down organizations and closed off from feedback from the public and from classroom practice. The only inward flow of communication occurs through personalized and individual contacts. Lower-level petitions occasionally get the attention of senior officials who are friends of friends, in other words, they work through clientele with well-placed officials.

Think global, act local 1: engagement with the base

All the third sector organizations we have looked at that work directly in the schools and, above all, in the classrooms with parents and the wider community have strong grass-roots bases. However, some grass-roots organizations transform into larger representative bodies, either to share activities or to build a constituency, the better to influence educational practice and occasionally even policy. The CNEII and MITEB in their heyday fell into this category.

Although there is considerable diversity in the membership and in other aspects among these 'deep activist' third sector organizations, two broad characteristics are shared by all of them: their responsiveness to the 'learning communities' they serve and their drawing on broad, national and international movements and intellectual and socio-political currents of thought. The teachers' third sector organizations emerged from the older social movements such as the SNTE, which means that the union is an official not a representative body.

In this respect, they belong to the kind of new social movements that Manuel Castells (1996), and Alain Touraine (1971) have identified. Touraine's 'new social movements' are distinguished by the way they reach beyond the workplace and the locality to the broader social spaces of the modern lifestyle of consumption, identity and governance. When teachers move from an exclusive concern for their pay and conditions and begin identifying themselves with the educational concerns of their 'learning community', they have entered the realm of the new social movements. The teachers' strike of 1989 and more recent civil disobedience in Zacatecas have been examples of teachers acting in conjunction with or alongside parents on issues of educational provision.

Some of the third sector organizations, especially those in indigenous areas, link with broader movements at local level. The 'Christian Base Communities' is an example. Other third sector organizations later adopted this term, as for example, Bases Magisteriales, in Jalisco. The educational organizations linked with the Zapatista movement see themselves as part of these broad social movements, which have local, national and international connections. The third sector organizations that involve parents and the community in the sharing and dissemination of best practice are by definition part of broad-based citizens' movements in favour of educational transformation. Although groups like ACUDE and Incidencia Civica en Educación have sprung out of school-based actions – such as the formation of student councils and civic projects in the community – their national and international networking, appealing to educational consumers, makes them part of the international movements in which the public takes on a single issue by entering a public space formerly the preserve of government officials. This points to a 'citizenization' of politics.

If the common feature of the third sector organizations is their dual reference to local concerns and international movements, what distinguishes them is their social class base. In the case of educators working with indigenous communities they address issues of mother tongue language use and include indigenous knowledge and cultural expression in their work. This is principally among marginal, rural communities, where a large proportion of the indigenous people live, and who most suffer the consequences of the 'one-size-fits-all' mainstream education on offer throughout the country. Most commonly, the leaders of the indigenous educational organizations are highly educated teachers or academics, many of whom are not indigenous themselves. They are examples of Gramsci's (1971) organic intellectuals bridging the gap between the local and the global.

Think global, act local 2: the international reach of local educational reconstruction

The linking of local action with international organizations is most clearly seen in the Base Communities in Chiapas that through their links with the activist Archbishop Samuel Ruiz managed to gain strong international support. A wide range of local organizations dealing with such areas as agriculture, indigenous languages and health were organized to achieve social justice in conditions of marginalization and official neglect, similar to the Brazilian Movimento dos Trabalhadores Rurais Sem Terra (MST). Some of the most wide-ranging educational organizations like the CNEII fitted this model.

Soon after its formation, the CNEII became one of the founder members of the United Nations Standing Committee on Indigenous Affairs. It also obtained financial support from the Ford Foundation and connections with senior personnel in the SEP. However, local groups, too, demonstrate this concern with international linkages, especially since, working independently of the formal educational bureaucracy, public funding is difficult to come by. Later, the Unidad de Investigación y Capacitación Educativa para la Participación (UCIEP), an umbrella organization also funded by international organizations, began lobbying the Senate to expand indigenous rights. These and similar indigenous TSOs have developed in the context of international and national concerns with discrimination against ethnic minorities and especially, First-Nation peoples. The SEP funds its own programmes and projects but rarely supports independent initiatives. Occasionally co-funding can occur where friendly official contacts are involved.

The INED (formerly the Casa de la Ciencia) began its life as a local museum in San Cristóbal de las Casa, and then through connections with El Colegio de la Frontera Sur (ECOSUR), it grew into a resource centre and eventually into a training centre for teachers, to a large extent because of untiring fund-raising with international agencies, and networking with the SEP and with other third sector organizations. At regional level in Chiapas, INED built a pluralistic TSO with a wide range of local groups all working on parallel educational projects in the region. This enabled both a learning community and a body of people to advance grass-roots educational work through collective effort.

A notable feature of citizen-based third sector organizations is that their very *raison d'être* is to develop extensive networks and systems of communication for their members as well as coordinating common activities, outward communications and events. The educational citizens' organizations in Mexico cover almost the whole political spectrum, though not as a single organization. On the left are organizations like the CNEII, ACUDE and ICE, although these do include a wide range of liberal interests. On the right are Mexicanos Primero and their constituent organizations. The middle ground is perhaps best represented by the quasi-governmental organizations, most especially OCE whose channels of communication are most used by the educated middle class. Like the indigenous and teachers' third sector organizations they are based around middle-class activists such as the leaders of the indigenous and teachers' groups. However, the information they provide is used by teachers and indigenous organizations working at base level to inform the parents and children of the state schools that they support.

Another category of citizens' organizations that takes advantage of broad ready-made networks are the religious organizations. The radical Catholic Church in Latin America is known for its active commitment to social justice. Although its relations with the government have more often than not been difficult, if not hostile, it can still mobilize hugely effective networks. These include priests and other church leaders, global networks, processes of dissemination through all types of media and the churchgoing public, often themselves organized in groups. The most visible are the Base Communities, which also have local networks through parallel secular or ecumenical organizations. All the different types of citizens' organizations count on the support of independent professionals, such as social workers, lawyers and journalists.

The teachers' third sector organizations have a distinctive way of networking. Because teachers are usually members of the 1.5 million strong corporative union, their professional links to the world beyond the school community are exclusively those of the SNTE and the ruling parties to which the SNTE is directly or indirectly affiliated. As such, they have little experience with and/or the means of developing networks outside the teaching community. Comradeship and mutual support characterizes teachers' lives over the often long (double-shift) working day, and over 30 or more years of working life. The lifetime tenure that all teachers aspire to and the majority have obtained, has, until recently, strengthened these bonds.

These values persist even when the teachers disassociate themselves from the comfort zone of the mainstream and mould themselves into the kinds of dissident groups discussed here. What marks off these third sector organizations from the mainstream teachers' organizations is that they work as a team in pedagogical as in more general organizational matters. The third sector organizations aim to develop collective teaching strategies through reflection, sharing ideas and experiences, and in the most ambitious cases, actually coordinating teaching throughout the educational careers of the students and their progression through the school grades. Such a student-centred, long-term approach to teaching is absent in the mainstream educational system.

Working towards educational emancipation: A contested terrain

The third sector organizations draw upon a vast body of ideas concerned with the complex relationship between official and local pedagogies and the idea that both the content and the form of educational programmes are at the heart of emancipation through education. In Europe, many nineteenth-century and early twentieth-century pedagogues like Célestin Freinet (1993) stressed the importance of learning being framed by the participants' own categories and experiences, and enquiry-based and cooperative learning. With the development of vast and inclusive national systems of education by the 1960s, this developed into questioning the form, content and value of conventional schooling. An example of this was Ivan Illich's concept of 'deschooling society' (1971). In Latin

America, Paulo Freire's pioneering work in developing alternative pedagogies and his strategies for reducing illiteracy encapsulated the various studies undertaken largely in Europe.

Against this background third sector organizations defined their task as starting with what we can call an internal transformation, consisting of both the teachers' reflection on their daily teaching practices and their commitment towards their charges, as well as to the needs and aspirations of the parents. Here they identify a fundamental contradiction between their classroom experience and the dictates of the authorities and the system. The teachers' third sector organizations found themselves caught in the middle of this. As state functionaries, they had the assigned task of delivering a prescriptive and rigid set of contents. At the same time, they engaged on a daily basis with pupils and parents for whom this content and the form of presentation not only did not correspond to their perceived needs, circumstances and aspirations but also 'interrupted' their systems of knowing. Cowen and Shenton (2003), as a result of their research into economic and social development policies, focused on the tension between these external controls and what they called 'the intrinsic learning impulses of students'.

The concept of external development refers to the deliberate intention of a particular authority to control the direction of the society and organize its resources. Behind this lies the notion that the government is the architect of social change through its enactment of policy. It is seen as an honest broker supposedly transcending all interests, although its architecture is one that connects with the dominant social classes. It justifies itself as the trustee of social welfare by casting the underprivileged as lacking dynamism and motivation and as needing government support. Victorian British politicians mesmerized by social Darwinism and the beginnings of eugenics considered the working class as demoralized and dispirited. Indigenous peoples in Mexico are treated similarly, though in this case their deficit is seen as racial destiny. In the educational sphere children are cast as unruly or feckless, a condition that only the state can rectify through social intervention, notably through schooling. Against these kinds of submission to external domination, Cowen and Shenton (2003) direct our attention to the much-neglected internal dimension of human beings' intrinsic impulses and ability to learn.

Many teachers' third sector organizations, as well as the activists in most of the others, have developed a response to this. To begin with the pedagogical aspects, these organizations reject performance-based approaches of recent reforms. As one of the coordinators of the CNEII said in its conference in the UPN, Mexico City in 2012, and echoed by other activists: '[t]esting has become the curriculum, and this is the wrong way round, and damaging for learning'. Rather than performance driving the curriculum, and summative evaluation informing educators when it is too late to make the necessary adjustments to learning, they place comprehension first. The students and teachers develop the capabilities of critical thinking in their learning rather than just following instructions and absorbing preset knowledge.

Their members also reject what they term as a 'one-size-fits-all' curriculum. They see this as endorsing a standardized profile of what a Mexican citizen should be, ignoring as a result, the diversity of the population and negating, for example, original languages and cultures. The alternative begins with the child's education in the home and community (most notably for example in the 'learning nests') and builds outwards to embrace the wider world, but always preserving the local social contexts. As such, learning is both broader and takes into account the whole range of interrelationships that a child develops at local, national and international levels. It is deeper because it starts with the child's realities, the child having a direct and intrinsic relationship with that learning. The child owns it and is intrinsically motivated to continue learning rather than depending on external stimuli.

According to these activists, and the parents and children they serve, the biggest obstacle to educational progress is not just authoritarianism but also neglect and the perfunctory, haphazard way education is provided, in large part because of the domination of personal politics and cronyism over formal commitments, resulting in an arbitrary and erratic educational delivery. This is why the third sector organizations emphasize that they are simply doing what the SEP is failing to do, rather than just offering a completely different programme of studies: refocusing attention on the school and the child. This is the basis of their radicalism; taking seriously the child-centred rhetoric of the official programmes, which for them implies releasing teachers (and pupils) from routine, time-wasting box-ticking activities and curriculum coverage in favour of a discovery learning approach.

They seek to build from classroom knowledge and experience upwards and outwards through this pedagogical model. The source of this process is the 'learning community', reflecting on actual practice, in the light of leaders sharing their knowledge and research on international best teaching practice. A MITEB leader put it in the following way:

> Our approach is to improve teaching through encouraging the teachers to learn through trial and error until they find what works for them in the conditions of the classroom and in relation to the kids they have in front of them. Then we share regularly our experiences in groups of reflection. Surely this is better than blindly applying pre-set regulations sent down from people who have never worked in a classroom.

The CENB leadership have been researching the factors that promote or impede pedagogical transformation. They believe that the chief obstacle to improved teaching is the lack of time and the opportunity to learn from experience.

Critical pedagogies

The principal challenge that critical pedagogies make to official educational doctrines is that knowledge cannot be deposited or 'banked' in children by a prescribed, one-size-fits-all curriculum. Knowledge, according to the approaches the third sector organizations follow, is generated out of the instinct to learn, from experience and through interactions with people and the physical world. This knowledge then consists of material transactions with nature, social interactions between people, social structure per se (such as economic structures) and personal reflections.

It is common to hear teachers criticize the prescriptive curriculum and the lack of critical thinking among their pupils. Nevertheless, the instruction-based learning that they received in their teachers' colleges, as well as the pressure the authorities put on teachers to cover the curriculum in its entirety, makes it difficult for teachers to inspire independent thought and puts at risk their learning. However, this is what the teachers' third sector organizations attempt to do. They take seriously constructivist lines of thought pervading academic centres and seminars for professional educators as well as earlier approaches to child-centred learning.

An example of such a child-centred approach grew out of the INED's resource centre where experts work directly with teachers on courses and *in situ.* In science education, teachers were encouraged to develop experimental situations in which children learn from experience. In one case, the children, literally getting their hands dirty through touching and kneading different materials, learn about viscosity and the transformation of their properties in different states. Art and theatre were also taught in order for the students to develop expressive abilities; and in indigenous communities, the students learn the different approaches to mathematics in Western, and in their own, cultures. The Mixe professor of the UPN in Oaxaca, Isaias Aldáz, conducted pioneering research in this area.

In order to give parents an increased voice in the school, the CENB began to invite them into classrooms to share their knowledge and skills in such areas as the production of educational materials, sharing their knowledge of the history and geography of their region. Parents also fed back their ideas and opinions on the school's work. The MITEB has increasingly seen the parents and community as central to their mission, involving them in the children's school projects. The parents have responded by supporting the teachers in their recent protests against the latest round of education reforms that they understand as interfering with the new approaches to formative learning that the MITEB has been developing. Involving parents and the community is particularly rooted in the indigenous TSOs. Tatutsi had its origins in the expressed wish of parents to have regular assemblies in which they guide the school's work. Indeed, the head teacher's role became that of a traditional *Wixarika* authority, in that he or she is obliged to take decisions consensually with the whole school community. The assembly as a basic form of public consultation and decision making has become a key area in the development of indigenous education.

Another example of an educational innovation that involves people not normally associated with schools is that of the language nests operating from the homes of grandmothers in the northern highlands of Oaxaca. Rather than children being located away from their home and cultural environment and placed in the alien environment of the school, the language nests begin the learning process in homes where the mother tongue is still spoken with their grandparents. Mothers who have begun to lose their mother tongue are and continue to be integrated into the programme. As the children grow they are increasingly introduced to the national and international curriculum, but starting from a strong grounding in their own culture. The ECIDEA, a group working in the highlands of Chiapas, has the same approach, starting with the indigenous cosmovision of the area, then introducing official knowledge with the aim of producing a new, integrated learning experience similar to the ethno-mathematics of Aldáz (1998).

Contracorriente supports projects in remote regions of Puebla, often with high outmigration. One of its signature programmes is the TV secondary schools in the Sierra Negra, where an officially recognized project-based learning approach is applied to local development issues. In one region, the students conduct research into the roots of alcoholism in the area and how to tackle it. A sister programme involves the *Tamachtini* TV secondary schools of a whole school zone in northern Puebla. Here school projects include workshops producing bread, traditional pottery and the cultivation of garlic with special advice from agricultural experts linked to the programme.

In Oaxaca, the community secondary schools located in indigenous areas and supported by the CMPIO, in consultation with the community, have designed a course of study that is entirely focused on local knowledge and dispositions. The schools reject standards and standardized forms of qualification, considering them to be irrelevant to the proper purpose of educating the young with respect for their cultures and their needs. Unlike the ECIDEA they do not combine traditional (local) with official knowledge to produce a new, broader learning programme. This places them in a situation whereby the students leave their schools without qualifications recognized by mainstream institutions, thereby limiting their mobility and life chances outside their localities. In some communities, up to half the population is living and working abroad and there are hardly any families that do not rely on remittances from their overseas relatives. Clearly the purpose of the curriculum tailored to life in the locality is to try to generate local opportunities. Yet trying to operate against strong economic forces through educational persuasion (see also Foster, 1965, and Martin, 2004) and attempts to reverse this trend through restricting the preparation of the young for possible lives in other settings have been counterproductive. Typically, they end up providing an education that is considered second class in the national context, thereby consigning those taking it to a second-class status. An alternative curriculum is therefore a risky venture and casts doubt upon the motives of those who promote it. The option taken by ECIDEA and Tatutsi of integrating traditional, culturally specific contents into the mainstream curriculum, not only avoids these risks but also may even prove to be a better preparation for students.

Educators and the learning community

The three main types of third sector organizations: the teachers' collectives, the indigenous associations and the citizens' organizations have different approaches to the construction of learning communities. Firstly, the teachers' organizations see the essence of their work as pedagogical and didactic, focusing on critical reflection of their work as a group in order to try, test and transform their teaching away from what they see as the staid prescriptiveness of conventional teaching and learning. Because parents, as seen in the last chapter, traditionally have been treated as passive recipients of their children's education, the third sector organizations have only slowly found ways to involve them more closely in the processes. Nevertheless, there are important examples of parental involvement, as in the CENB and the MITEB.

Secondly, promoting parental participation in their children's education is part of the main purpose of citizens' third sector organizations, notably the ACUDE and the ICE. They aim to make official education more responsive to its users rather than to particular interest groups that tend to filter, control and stratify access. The ACUDE and component members of ICE have their roots in school-based projects. In the early 2000s ACUDE helped develop a children's school board in a poor neighbourhood on the outskirts of Mexico City. From this type of involvement and with a large network of organizations carrying out similar work, ACUDE has been building their campaigns for a democratic education at national level. Most members are educators or educational researchers and activists. However, not all are teachers, and even though closer relationships with independent teachers' organizations exist, the emphasis in the work is on giving a voice to parents, children, the school community and the public at large and encouraging them to play a more active role than is customary.

The indigenous associations almost by definition emphasize their rootedness in the community and the parents. All the indigenous third sector organizations draw from the indigenous world views of the schools in which they work – the idea that education is a seamless part of the socialization of the child from birth through schooling and beyond. This explains why parents become so involved with the child's schooling and why they place such importance on assemblies as their preferred form of participation in educational matters.

A common response of the educational authorities when presented with innovative projects and programmes developed outside official SEP policy is to dismiss them as unimportant, small and unable to be scaled up. The SEP and SNTE are highly sensitive to autonomous educational initiatives, since they consider that public education is the business of the state, not civil society. Leaving aside the official hubris behind such responses, there is truth in the fact that many innovations never go beyond their immediate birthplace, because those working on them are too busy developing, honing and applying their innovations to extend their reach. They lack the networks and experience to promote their work. Yet for their work to survive, let along be scaled up, in an ethos of hostility towards independent action in the highly controlled and centralized setting of public education in Mexico, independent actions need the support of local, regional, national and international networks.

Indigenous organizations have proved better at this than the independent teacher organizations on the whole. The teachers, accustomed to their union groupings and local school-zone collectives, have not been able to reach out to external agencies. They have found it difficult to find a new home in an alternative fellowship or network. Many do have international connections, but these are not continually activated and rarely feed into and directly support their companions, especially when they are up against opposition from the government. However, most are aware of the importance of these networks to compensate for their estrangement from the SEP–SNTE nexus. Contracorriente has been especially active in its networking in order to take advantage of its university research connections, international migrant association networks and its communication and social media knowledge repositories.

The tension between their role as a state employee and their vocation to serve the community is well summed up in the phrase coined by the umbrella teachers' third sector organization, Educación y Cambio, 'Return the gaze to the classroom' (Cero en Conducta, 1985). An active Bases Magisteriales teacher explains how, when the local educational authority was pressuring teachers to persuade parents to buy crib sheets for upcoming tests, he was torn between his conscience that told him that the authority was taking advantage of parents and his solidarity with his peers who decided that objections from the teachers would prejudice the school at a later date. His Solomonic solution was buying the crib sheets for his own students with his own money.

An example of sustained thoroughgoing externalization of its work is the CNEII, at least during its more active period between 2000 and 2012. Rooted in a network of local indigenous groups working in education, the CNEII's regional and national meetings focused on exchanging experiences and agreeing on a protocol for working together in the future. Through contact with senior personnel in the SEP, a relationship was established with international funders to finance its activities. Later on, the CNEII members made contact with the legislature and canvassed representatives on the need to eradicate discrimination in education (i.e. with regards to general provision and language). From an increasingly nationwide network of indigenous educational groups, and with a presence in the legislative and executive arms of government, the CNEII began arranging meetings to share experiences of developing materials and deliver broad-based workshops in which national and international experts contributed. This is how the 'language nests' were developed. Furthermore, meetings were held to coordinate campaigns. One of these was a large anti-discrimination campaign organized throughout the country.

Another example demonstrates the two-way flow of externalization and learning feedback to the organization. This was the campaign to take the SEP to court for discrimination against indigenous pupils through testing and teaching in the second language, Spanish, in areas where the mother tongue was indigenous. This campaign started with just one committed head teacher and a set of parents and teachers. After a long legal battle in which the CNEII was the chief coordinator, the teachers and parents eventually won the case before the National Commission on Anti-Discrimination (CONAPRED) and an official court of justice. This combination of actions brought to public awareness a renewed purpose in education, in this case, the legally established right of all children to education in any of the national languages. It pointed to the routine flouting of this law, and won a legal victory that can serve as a precedent.

This conveys only a small part of the overall vision and intention of indigenous education, even though many more conflicts and disputes in the same field were lost rather than won. Nevertheless, it demonstrates the power of national, local and international linkages in projecting a renewed educational purpose that challenges the comfortable status quo that the SEP is the dominant player in all matters concerning public education and has been failing in its purpose even on its own terms. The achievements of CNEII still fall short: there is a long way to go before indigenous or other learning communities can determine their educational programmes within the public system (some have already done so outside it). Although CONAPRED charged the complainants together with the CGEIB to examine and recommend measures to attack discrimination in other areas of education, political opposition and foot-dragging soon brought this process to a halt.

Victories for the third sector organizations can be pyrrhic too. Tatutsi eventually succeeded in obtaining support for its intercultural school with teachers eventually being paid by the authorities. However, this success brought with it the cost of having to bring contents and teaching into line with standardized SEP requirements, and to cede control over school policy to the SEP. Others have fought similar battles. The teachers' third sector organizations have relied more on contacts inside the SEP, or university staff, especially those in the National Pedagogic University. The MITEB grew in the conjuncture of two left-of-centre governments in Zacatecas that drew in senior educators and UPN academics. These organizations negotiated spaces for MITEB to develop its radical reflexive in-service teacher training that eventually went national. Learning communities developed through continuous pedagogical innovation and parental involvement to the point where the schools in which the MITEB has been most active are recognized as being of superior quality. With the change in government in 2010, MITEB was orphaned and its members beat a retreat to the UPN.

An alternative vision

The central point about this alternative vision and practice of education is that not only is it based on purely educational rather than political criteria but also that in uniting rather than separating educational objectives from its users, it legitimates itself by attempting to find ways in which the power of contextualization based upon local knowledge can be released to emancipate the individual from what holds him or her back. The alternative could well be to examine the educational experiences of models closer to home, namely those carried out by the independent organizations that have been the subject of this chapter. The third sector organizations in Mexico, as with similar independent ones elsewhere, developed out of the frustrations of local educational stakeholders with the incomplete and inequitable educational provision over the preceding decades. This radicalized an important part of the third sector organizations in Mexico, especially those working inside or close to the heart of the system of education, principally teachers and educators in poor areas. At the same time, their rules of operation limited the range and scope of their activities to little more than additions to official programmes and collaborations with the authorities to make up for shortfalls in or misappropriations of public expenditure. The net result has been mutual suspicion and even hostility on each side rather than a partnership in a more open regime of educational provision.

For their part, the 'deep activist' third sector organizations have learned to sidestep the authorities and disappear as much as they can from the authorities' panoptic gaze. In part, this has been achieved through the intervention of friends in high places; in part working on the margins of the official system and working from inside outwards; from the immanent characteristics of learning, rather than from the external intentions of the highly politicized doctrines of the authorities, filtered and drained of educational resolve by the time they reach the school.

Whilst this novel way of working in the Mexican context is not unknown in other parts of the world, in Mexico it is highly innovative and requires enormous inputs of thought, time and effort. It is fraught with tensions between practices, colleagues and operational styles. Yet the result is consistent with the cutting edge of innovative pedagogies promoted at international levels. The latter has included many of the third sector organizations in its register of world educational innovations. The new pedagogy and the democratic educational organization that surrounds it is lived in the microcosm of their area of influence like an oasis learning community, similar, as we have seen, to the post-revolutionary lifestyles Castells (1996) has described. In the last chapter of this book, we examine systems of education and how they change.

7
Systems and System Reforms

In the preceding chapters, we have focused on the history and structure of educational institutions, practices and outcomes in Mexico. We also set ourselves the task of trying to understand the nature and constitution of specific problems in the implementation of reforms. In particular, we have seen how proposed reforms of the curriculum, pedagogic approaches and processes of evaluation have repeatedly failed and how the training, role and function of teachers is so structured that they can rarely function as reliable agents for government-initiated educational programmes and policies. We have seen that teachers more often than not are part of a complex process that blocks such changes and innovations; and how parental involvement designed to create a more communicative model has been marginalized. Finally, we examined how proposed reforms that emerge from civil groups and community actions are consistently frustrated. We contextualized our discussion by looking at the history of the system and found that for complex socio-historical and cultural reasons, education in Mexico is more concerned with control and the maintenance of social order than it is with learning. We suggested that a very complicated interplay between formal and informal factors is at work. It is this relationship that we now examine in greater depth.

In Chapters 1 and 2 we laid out the theoretical, methodological and socio-historical foundations for an understanding of the key elements of education by examining the notion of a system and the development of educational institutions and practices in their socio-historical contexts. In Chapter 3 we looked at the development of the curriculum, that is, a planned programme of learning, pedagogic and assessment reforms and the assumptions that lie behind them. In Chapter 4 we focused on teacher training, both pre- and in-service. We concluded that the gap between policy intentions and their instantiations consists not just of material conditions but also of very important and little studied informal relationships, which the Mexicans sardonically call *compadrazgo* or clientelism. They both pervade and often override formal educational structures.

In Chapter 5 we looked at parental and community participation in schools. We found that the educational authorities have long acted like *caciques* (best understood as 'political bosses') of state education, treating it almost feudally as their exclusive domain, with the justification that they are obliged to civilize and control a diverse and economically and socially unequal population. This has engendered a culture of silence among the mass of the population, grateful for the opportunity for their children to study, but by no means content with the educational services they receive. Policies to encourage greater participation are not enacted and will remain so as long as parents feel they risk more by involving themselves in what the teachers see as their domain. Teachers cannot be blamed entirely for not responding to and collaborating with parents, given the onerous, unpredictable and bureaucratic conditions in which they work. The result is a divorce of convenience between the school and the community.

In Chapter 6 we examined alternatives to current institutions and practices with a focus on pedagogy and community involvement in education. These projects tend to occur on the fringes of the system, where vigilance is weakest, and where authority figures share the project teachers' idealism to create a more democratic, child-centred education. They are strengthened by parental and community support and are often linked locally with radical innovations in other sectors such as agricultural cooperatives and popular forms of governance. They draw on past radical traditions and newer approaches closer to the new social movements studied by Castells (1996) and Touraine (1971).

It is important to emphasize that in the course of our explorations we have raised problems that are both theoretical and perhaps even more importantly, practical. Two themes are ever present in our presentation of the evolution and structure of education in Mexico. The first is the relationship between formal and informal elements and procedures in the development of policy and practice at all levels of education. The second is the need to understand the origin and function of established systems of education so that reforms can have a greater chance of succeeding.

In Chapter 1 we pointed out that traditional systems theory as discussed by some of the older functionalist social scientists, and in contemporary interdisciplinary circles, depends on the establishment of boundaries. If we are inclined to view the educational system as discrete and bounded, we are likely to exclude vital elements that influence its real functioning, that is, we neglect informal relationships. These are not of the same order as the formal bureaucratic arrangements the educational system is normally understood to have, not least because they are specific to the society in which the formal arrangements operate.

Formal and informal elements

It is clear from the history of education in Mexico that the determinants of educational policies and practices are a complex and interacting set of factors rooted in the wish to preserve and maintain a system of social control. We have characterized this as the interplay between the formal and the informal, that is, between established institutional procedures and practices of the official system and the various practices of clientelism and cronyism that vitiate all levels of decision making in the system.

Our discussion of the formal and informal and the complex relations between them will focus on the teacher. Hence, a recurrent part of this work is that we do not forget that in decision-making processes the rigidness of formal structures and processes often means that decisions are made through parallel and, most confusingly, sometimes through overlapping informal structures. In countries like Mexico the informal can easily override, if not replace, the formal structure. Mexican researchers are not encouraged to investigate this area and the opaqueness of its procedures often makes it difficult to understand what is happening. International practitioners, analysts and comparativists have even less capacity to understand the problem. They are hampered because they restrict themselves to working with the formal system. They therefore concentrate on the formal aspects, regarding them, by default, as being synonymous with what they call the education system.

As we have seen in Chapters 2 and 4, the results of 70 years of single-party rule, with very little changing during the 12-year period when the presidency was occupied by another party, has been the establishment of educational institutions and practices hallmarked by opaqueness in decision making and procedures, clientelism and a lack of accountability, underwritten by a misuse of public funds. The development of a trade unionism more concerned with graft and maintaining social control rather than any real commitment to education – combined with a prebendalist bureaucracy – has made educational imperatives subservient to the maintenance of the system. In the eyes of international organizations, Mexico's educational policies, on paper, appear to be rational, progressive and open, to a fault. The upshot has been decades of educational inertia, reflected recently in the past 17 years of Mexico remaining among the worst performing countries in the PISA league tables (for example, see also Ornelas (2008, 2012, 2014), Barba (2010) and Posner et al. (2017)).

It is important to emphasize that until now there has been little discussion of the process by which the authorities exercise their almost exclusive control and how the administration has bound together the variety of component institutions that make up the educational system. On paper the organizational chart looks similar to that of any other educational system. But this belies its real daily operation and it is in the grey area between the official version of educational procedures and what actually happens that we find out how the system operates. In reality, we have a vast and overarching network of interpersonal relations among individual teachers, bureaucrats and authorities to whom teachers are beholden through the interchange of favours and loyalty. The influence these authorities exercise is not necessarily derived from their functions in the bureaucratic hierarchy. More commonly, their power is as a result of their political influence. Indeed, this type of informal network frequently traverses the formal chain of command in most educational processes. This almost invisible and informal clientelist system at the heart of the education administration has encouraged not only cronyism but also corruption in the conduct of educational activities at all levels. The tendency has been not to blame the system but to castigate the teachers for its continued failure. This charge of culpability more than any other element weighs heavily upon the teaching profession that has had little or no responsibility for the creation of a system more concerned with social control than with stimulating the development of an actively inquisitive population. Moreover, the process of decision- and policy-making at each level is complex and often serpentine. For example, as we have seen at the national level, complicated and convoluted negotiations take place between the most powerful stakeholders, such as religious and entrepreneurial organizations *and* the SNTE and the ruling party.

As policy is filtered down through the system it is subject to other pressures. In relatively weak systems of control there is room for other actors, such as parents, community leaders, teachers themselves as well as established political and trade union organizations, to take part. The labyrinthine nature of the process has yet to be fully analysed in the Mexican context. We can point to James Scott's (2010) study of anti-centralized state formations in Southeast Asia; Bruno Latour's (1987) examination of real laboratory activity as distinct from the formal and taken-for-granted idea of the 'scientific method'; Mary Douglas' (2002) concepts of ritual purity and pollution in different societies and times; the social anthropologist, Gerald Mars' (1982) revealing research on informal work practices; and even more relevantly, Merilee Grindle's (1977) investigation into Mexican bureaucrats in a food assistance programme. Despite this gap in the literature, these works can act to guide our endeavours.

Teachers and teaching

Teachers are expected to transmit policy through their classroom activities. The degree of autonomy that a teacher in the classroom has largely depends on the relative strength of a number of factors. These include: the extent to which control over the curriculum and pedagogy filters down to the classroom; the complex relationship between the state and local education authorities and the federal government; the type of control exerted by the head teacher; the degree to which the teacher is involved in or subject to the complex web of political control and beholden to patronage that is exerted at all levels of the system; the degree to which the school is loosely or strongly coupled to the system; and the degree to which the school figures on the antennae of the authorities. The relationship between these six elements largely determines their degree of autonomy in the classroom.

A good example of the informal system and its consequences is a comparison between official norms relating to the school calendar and how it is used in the schools. The school day is scheduled to last for four and a half hours (the majority of schools operating on a shift system means that time is limited), 30 minutes of which is for recreation. Although this does not leave very much time for learning, the actual time given to learning in the classroom is even less, around two hours. In addition to the 200 school days that include holidays and monthly teacher meetings, the schools suspend classes for a variety of reasons not included in the official calendar. There are local feast days, preparation for parades (the parades themselves are other days lost from the school calendar), various competition days and adverse weather conditions (in some areas even normal rainfall causes the suspension of classroom activities). In recent years the SEP has made much of teachers needing to plan their classes; they are expected to develop long-term plans and be seen to be doing so. The mere presentation of a plan should not be confused with actual lesson preparation. Furthermore, these plans are rarely checked to see if they have been implemented. Observations in classrooms in Jalisco indicate that there is a chasm between these plans and the way teachers cover the curriculum. Their many ancillary activities make it impossible to plan ahead – they operate on a day-to-day basis.

What should be a routine exercise of complying with official planning demands, itself displaces both lesson preparation time and, frequently, actual teaching time. Up to the end of the 1990s there was virtually no formal assessment of students and teachers. Then, in the early 2000s the pendulum swung in the opposite direction, largely motivated by the Mexican government's desire to be seen to attempt to raise its performance in the international league tables. A whole raft of high-stakes tests was launched in 2000. All these expensive and time-consuming exercises have not had much impact on student attainment as measured by the PISA evaluations; indeed, in the 2013 OECD report Mexico's aggregate performance regressed. A costly investment in evaluation can have a negative effect on learning, as other studies have noted (see also Scott 1985, 2010). Among other outcomes is that standardized aptitude testing (SAT) has replaced learning with a regime of teaching to the test.

Another series of demands on teachers is invisible. It includes all the informal pressures on teachers' time to sustain and develop their careers. In order to understand them, we need to think in terms of two interrelated and interactional frameworks. The first one is the official chain of command of departments in federal and state secretariats of education. At the top of this chain of command is the Secretary of Education and at the bottom are the teachers. The second framework is a hierarchical network of interrelations between colleagues, superiors and subordinates. The interrelation between them is personal. Although this hierarchy normally mirrors that of the formal framework, it is different because some less important members of the formal system may have more influence in the informal system by virtue of their strong political connections at higher levels. The influence a superior has over his or her subordinates in the informal framework is more a question of personal political loyalty than it is about educational expertise; its currency is the giving and receiving of favours. The two systems do not easily coexist and it is the friction between them that accounts for much of the incoherence of educational processes.

In Chapter 1 we referred to the recent abolition of the Carrera Magisterial at the beginning of the current presidential administration in 2013, with it being replaced first by an Examen Periódico Universal and then by open competition consisting of a multiple choice examination and evaluations by superiors, supposedly based on the aspirant's quality of service. Plazas, as we suggested, are now being phased out. Although the vast majority of teachers currently in service are still holding plazas, they can be removed from service altogether if they fail an assessment or do not get assessed. Prior to the completion of their basic teacher training, most teachers found a tenured position through personal negotiations with senior personnel in the SEP–SNTE structure. This was typically brokered through intermediate figures in the hierarchy. Currently, with the advent of national testing, the union has been excluded from its once crucial role in teacher placement. This reform in service conditions is an example of the formal system working in opposition to the informal system and, in this case, acting to change the relationship between the formal and the informal elements of the system.

We will use two contrasting cases of the recent recruitment of two head teachers to illustrate the unexpected and disruptive consequences of this new policy. Francisco José is a bright young teacher who, after six years of teaching and a Masters degree, became a head teacher. The network that he established through his teaching experiences and higher degree studies was to play an important role in his career. He embarked on his new duties fully aware of potential opposition to the new legitimacy that his promotion represented. His approach was to attempt to be fair but firm, attacking what he saw as inefficiencies in the secondary school. This resulted in an exodus of several teachers who were near retirement and who felt uncomfortable under his leadership. Others tolerated the changes but resisted the considerable pressures to conform. A few accepted with grace the new situation. To make up for the retired teachers' withdrawal, he recruited new teachers in such a way as to maximize his new approach. His acquisition of new like-minded teachers owed much to his networks among colleagues in the Secretariat of Education in his state.

At the same time an experienced biology teacher, Ariel, in the secondary school where Francisco José became the head teacher, gained a similar head teacher position, also through the new regime. A wave of retirements followed. Ariel, too, faced a challenge of replacing teachers and support staff. Unfortunately, Ariel was less well connected than Francisco José. Not surprisingly, he found it more much difficult to recruit open-minded teachers as replacements and had to cover directorial and teaching responsibilities at the same time. Support from the authorities was not forthcoming and long-established teachers gave no help either. Ariel was left in an untenable position. On the one hand, he owed his position to the new system of examinations imposed by the authorities but on the other hand he did not have their support. After several months in this situation he became ill and at the end of the first year he felt he had no choice but to resign.

It might seem strange that the federal education authorities were reluctant to support the pioneers of one of their signature policies. Even more striking with regards to recruitment to headship was that the school and state authorities used the old clientelistic system in disregard of the new regulations. A good deal of this incompatibility between policy and practice has to do with the not always harmonious relations between the central and the state authorities. In their analyses of policy, Ornelas (2012) and Barba (2010) have demonstrated that where state governments are run by a different political party from the federal government or where the trade union is powerful enough at the state level to resist, the hiring, promoting and firing of teachers is frequently conducted at local levels. Hence, in some states where the SEP–SNTE preserved many of the old practices, the new measures did not come into effect. Our two head teachers exemplify this situation. In each case, but for different reasons, normal school routines were held captive to political considerations of a largely clientelistic nature.

The federal government has issued a string of directives to encourage schools to work in and with their communities. These activities frequently impinge on school time, sometimes for up to a month in advance, occupying entire school days. Time is devoted to the preparation of parades and organizing performances of dancers, singers and acrobats, as well as the routine marching that accompanies most school celebrations. There are other events like the Christmas' *posadas*, teachers' farewell get-togethers and seasonal celebrations, which are not recognized as official holidays. It is not clear whether the time used for such events should be subtracted from teaching hours or from some other unidentified period. Most schools operate on a double-shift system that means the only option is to sacrifice formal learning time.

There is a whole raft of informal incursions into the daily life of teachers. We have emphasized that time subtracted from classroom teaching for teachers to perform necessary but unscheduled, unexpected activities, as well as occurrences that diminish teacher's moral and emotional well-being, reduce the quality of education. This in turn is reflected in students' educational attainments. These factors are rarely recognized in policy discussions or even in the academic field, but are indicative of how a failing centralized system operates.

We need now to distinguish between service and work conditions, because this distinction constitutes the basis for much of our argument. By service conditions we mean the regulations that govern the way teachers are selected, hired, remunerated, promoted and given pensions, as well as their access to benefits and other career perks. These conditions are the most visible aspects of teachers' lives and the ones that most occupy discussions and cause confrontations with the authorities and among each other. Working conditions refer to aspects more directly related to the specific pedagogical interactions between teachers, students and, in some cases, their parents. Although these conditions compare unfavourably with other OECD countries and drew strong criticism from the independent Instituto Nacional de Evaluación Educativa (INEE), they rarely appear on the list of complaints made by teachers and in union negotiations with the authorities.

It is in the space between service and working conditions that the implementation of policies fails. However, analysts have had little to say about this crucial area. The government bias towards dealing with service conditions is reflected in the current reform that has been termed by many as a labour reform rather than an educational one (see also Posner et al., 2017). But over many decades, reforms have ground to a halt mired in disagreements about conditions of service. The educational community, policymakers, teachers, bureaucrats and even some researchers have lost their sense of direction about the purpose of education.

As we have seen, policy changes and new initiatives are attempted every six years with the change in government. Indeed, the current administration has exceeded this by making changes nearly every year. Aware of the federal government's inability or even lack of desire to monitor and police these changes, teachers have learned how to ride out these reform packages by mastering and repeating the latest government justifications but only making cosmetic adjustments to their teaching practices. By doing so they guarantee relative peace in the classroom and skilfully avoid demands that could, in their view, disrupt their work. They thus pay lip service to whatever change is the flavour of the year whilst continuing to operate as they did before, in order to avoid conflicting and certainly time-consuming demands.

Another confusion faced by novice teachers is the often abrupt changes in official policy explanations and in educational expectations. At one point trainee teachers were faced with 'objectives and aims' in their lesson planning, yet, a few years later in the classroom, the current fashion became what were called competences and the 'didactic situation'. As one teacher commented to us at a refresher course in 2014, when asked what he had learnt up to that moment, he said: 'all we have to do is to get to one o'clock without falling asleep; after all, in a few years' time they'll change all these and we'll have to learn it all again'.

We have so far described the influence of informal practices on formal educational time and space – how they override formal arrangements and yet how they are at the same time the process through which educational intentions are actually accomplished. We have cast this explanation in terms of two parallel frameworks, with the informal one compensating for and benefiting from the structural weaknesses of the formal one. Beyond the description we have given, we need to understand how it is that informal practices are able to take place even if these practices are legally irregular, even illicit and in some cases illegal. A way to understand this state of affairs is to identify the structural weaknesses in the formal educational system. These include gaps in regulations or areas that policy does not cover; inconsistencies or grey areas, that is, where there is ambiguity or where irregular actions are difficult to detect.

The weakness of the rule of law has in the last two decades become an important area of research in development studies. Rodrik (2008) has seen this as a major cause of corruption in developing countries. It includes both the poor implementation of the rules of the law and its absence in important affairs. The new approach to teacher evaluation is an example of the latter. Teachers are evaluated through a multiple choice examination, but their classroom work is left unexamined. This leaves teachers free to conduct themselves according to their own style, rather than being subject to guidance and correction.

These grey areas fall into two categories: a lack of definition or ambiguity in the rules and contradictions in the rules. An example of the former, which we have already pointed to, concerns the allocation of responsibilities between two shifts. Whilst the SEP has laid down guidelines in this matter, in practice these are difficult to follow and do not cover all the eventualities. A typical example is where two shifts share resources such as library books as part of the National Reading Programme. Library books allocated to a double-shift school remained in the boxes as a result of a dispute between the two shifts over their use and storage. There are also occasions when the rules contradict each other. An incongruity at the most fundamental level of Mexican public education involves the constitutional right of all children to free education. This was repudiated three years ago when the then Secretary of Education in Jalisco declared that parents could pay in kind if they did not have the money to pay registration fees. On a daily basis, parents are required to make contributions to school maintenance and for textbooks which until recently were free.

Grey areas or ambiguities and incongruences in the rules are not unique to Mexico. In other countries, like the United States, when there is disagreement, between, for example, the teachers' union, the school board and school district, arbitrators and legal specialists are frequently called in to resolve the issue. Such a situation is rooted in the fact that education in the United States evolved upwards from local communities, slowly and steadily involving more actors with different responsibilities in relation to each other. The Mexican problem is produced by an opposite tendency. Public education, as we have seen, came from the top and then progressed downwards. Many of the problems we have been discussing arise from the central authorities decanting responsibilities not just to lower levels of the system but also, more importantly, to informal political levels.

The third institutional weakness is immunity from any of the consequences of bending the rules. Those who do are protected by their patrons. Where the rules are broken without this protection, actions are interpreted as disloyalty and lead to penalties such as a withdrawal of support for clients' career ambitions. At the highest level, the best example of such an occurrence of a penalty paid for disloyalty was the dispossession of the goods of the last two national union leaders for perceived betrayal of the ruling party. It is not uncommon for official programmes to be sidelined at school level because the local authorities have other priorities. This has happened in Jalisco where the National Reading Programme has been largely inconsequential. A reliance on the informal system creates and sustains an institutional culture of arbitrariness that affects the whole institution. This naturally leads to blocking policy implementations and a diversion of resources.

The final form of institutional weakness occurs when irregular practices are invisible and thus cannot be detected. This is particularly common at the lowest levels of the educational system, notably among teachers themselves. In addition to being absent from the school, the teacher may be absent from their pedagogic duties during teaching time; a kind of invisible absence. Teachers often assign routine tasks that have little to do with the curriculum to pupils whilst surfing the Internet, filling in forms and attending to personal business. Teachers have conversations and meetings with colleagues during class time, which frequently interrupt important classroom activities.

The school is a great deal more than a collection of classrooms where teachers teach and children learn. Each school has its own unique ethos. School ethos refers to the formal and informal ways in which the teachers interact with each other, with pupils and with parents. New teachers quickly learn how to navigate through this ethos in such a way as to allow them to fit in. Since teachers may well spend many hours in their schools in close contact with their colleagues, this accommodation is an important part of their work. Occasionally, the camaraderie expected among members of the teaching body transgresses the strict tenets of ethical integrity. An example might be encouraging pupils to cheat in tests. New teachers have to learn their place in the hierarchical relations that constitute the life of the school.

Over the course of the first years of teaching, the new teachers may find themselves having to make fundamental decisions about the kind of teacher they would like to become. Stephen Ball (1994) focusing on teachers and their abilities as teachers in a very different environment, distinguished between swimmers, floaters or sinkers. In Mexico, social control rather than selection is the main element in judging whether a teacher is succeeding or not and the criteria that are being used often embrace ideological elements. For example, in Jalisco, as a result of complex political events, teachers frequently classified themselves as institutional or dissident, according to how far they distanced themselves from party or union politics. These political definitions have ethical underpinnings, in that affiliations with the official institutions often require teachers to subordinate their classroom duties to political and administrative imperatives. By contrast, some groups of dissidents prioritize the pedagogical aspects of their work and in so doing are seen as outsiders or dissidents. Other dissidents such as those of the Coordinadora may well share with the Institutionalists a pragmatic approach to teaching. Not all teachers can be placed in these categories; many keep a low profile, teach without enthusiasm and opt for the quiet life.

Teachers have to cope with ever more frequent changes to their service and working conditions with very little consultation and with even less support from their trade union. Hence, another and potentially more serious example is perfunctorily paying homage to a new curriculum or set of teaching methods whilst in reality continuing with older approaches that the teacher is more comfortable with. This fits with what Gerald Mars (1982) in his pioneering study called cheating at work. It can take the form of passive resistance. Other writers have examined this nascent opposition to the system and its practices in which teachers have only a diminished role; for example, Fullan and Hargreaves (1996) and Gonzalez-DeHass et al. (2005). This is how teachers survive in a system where formal institutions and processes are much less powerful than those that are informal.

Education systems

When the activities of the state expanded into economic and social management, models of policy development and implementation, and psychological/business management that emphasize incentives the state could use to influence behaviour, were widely adopted. These approaches implicitly or explicitly take as given that the public sector has the capacity to act coherently as a unity in order to implement policies. Some versions of each take more or less seriously the recipients of policies by modelling typical behaviours, but these recipients are treated more as active respondents than as authors of change. The psychological models have been more associated with the business sector but have been applied in the public sector too, and tend to assume the malleability of behaviour according to incentives, again treating policy recipients as objects rather than subjects of change.

However, the Mexican state continued to play an important role in social control. The expanded state generated entire social strata that depended directly on it for their existence as well as the accumulation of the kinds of social capital that would guarantee their existence. Equally, the state's role varied greatly from one society to the next. As a result, we find that two other approaches were developed: sociological and anthropological studies of bureaucracies and institutions, and political and political-economic analyses of the state and its development. These approaches questioned the primacy of the state in relation to other forces for change.

It has been argued that a policy regime, in the sense that Michael Burawoy (2009) originally used it in his analysis of production regimes and in particular Fordism, expresses its legitimate trusteeship over society through an image of the guiding principle for how society should be organized. This, for example, could be the concept of the invisible hand of the market, so fondly used in Britain since the Thatcherite era, or the protection of national identity in India (*'bharata mem rastriya pahacana'*). The particular doctrine and its application in policy development and implementation can give us an idea of the regime's fault lines and the kinds of problems and contradictions it is likely to have to face up to.

We therefore need to examine how the state has been classified and categorized into types. Cowen and Shenton (2003) developed a typology that consisted of: a laissez-faire regime, a segmented protectionist regime, a corporative-clientelist regime, a developmentalist regime and a social democratic regime. The first of these is the laissez-faire regime.

Here, the authority source for the state draws upon the invisible hand of the market. For more than 30 years Anglo-Saxon countries have followed this path, ordering not only the economy but also, to various degrees, their social sectors, emphasizing the idea of consumer choice. As we will see further on, this policy has had a profound impact on education policy. Although it is claimed all citizens are equal before the market and laws that protect them, in fact this rarely operates as it is intended. This has resulted in a continuous struggle between equality and corporate interests.

Nation building in least developed countries (LDC) has in many cases entailed economic protectionism. This is accompanied by political and cultural protectionism, a zealous resistance to external influences, protecting their national sovereignty from powerful nations, such as the USA and European countries, and the defence of a rediscovered or newly invented common history and culture. We might want to describe this as a segmented protectionist regime. This has generated notions of underdevelopment and the appeal to forms of national development that are more autochthonous in opposition to Western influences. Not all national integration has relied on corporativism, though patron-clientage has been widespread. In democratic countries with large and diverse populations, the state draws upon a shared sense of tradition or an ancient culture. At the same time it acknowledges in law and government the plural nature of society, such as in countries as diverse as India, South Africa and Brazil. In this category, the trade-off between the state and civil society is different from laissez-faire regimes, in that challenges to the central government are commonplace. In this type of regime, protectionism in the social sector may coexist with liberalization of the economy.

The third of our types is the corporative-clientelist regime. Whilst generally working within a capitalist framework, corporativist systems are largely governed by centralized institutions, where social, political and economic power is shared among various competing groups, none of which achieve dominance over the others. Economic aims are ultimately sacrificed to maintaining social cohesion and whilst private enterprises are often dominant within the process of decision making, many of their aims become attenuated and, indeed, sacrificed in order to maintain social order. The system is based on compromises worked out by the elites of the hitherto competing sectors. Its weakness is that it is basically unacceptable to those who work within it because such a socio-political arrangement entails their own policies and policy implementations being marginalized and ultimately set aside in order to avoid conflict. Promotion is achieved through networking, usually funnelled through a single agency like a political organization and its ancillaries, which in liberal democratic societies would be called corruption. Most emerging economies have gone through periods of nation building to integrate diverse and fragmented populations into a unity for economic and political reasons. Mexico is an example of a country that has sought a sense of national identity through corporate vertical integration (i.e. official unions and chambers of commerce, etc.). In this way, extreme social conflict has been pre-empted, but this has resulted in the sacrificing of efficiency in the name of patrimonial loyalties.

The fourth of our models is the developmentalist state. In contrast to the early industrializing nations like the United Kingdom, where the state responded to economic entrepreneurship, in the later industrializers in the Far East, the state anticipated and fomented it. This was sometimes conducted through government protectionism and subsidies to business. For all of the recent industrializers the state plays a central role in promoting development. Even in a clientelist rentier state, like Mexico, the business community and national and even more so international offshore companies enjoyed subsidies, tariffs and privileged tax concessions, especially in the boom years between the 1940s and late 1970s.

Rather than acting as the authority over economic and social development, here the state established a reciprocal relationship with business; providing subsidies in return for high economic performance. The latter was to be achieved by borrowing cutting-edge technologies from the West principally, and applying them to the increasingly multi-purpose enterprises of the region. The expert engineer was the hero of this scenario, driven most especially, and most relevantly, by mass education. In the developmentalist state, education precedes development, rather than following it; its funding being contingent on economic growth. Two consequences follow from the technological targeting approach to state support for business. The first is that the emphasis on performance reduces the scope for clientelism that so characterizes clientelist states' relationships to business and services. The second is that the emphasis on learning, or technological borrowing, places a premium on education as the precondition for development. As such, it is supported, and invested in, by governments, particularly in relation to teacher professionalization, thereby encouraging adaptability and commitment to keeping pace with technological advances. This therefore leaves little room for factional interests subverting the drive for increasing educational attainment.

In the last of our types, the social democratic regime, the state presides over a more egalitarian and participative citizenry, drawing its authority from claims of inclusiveness, broad participation (e-government, referendums, etc.) and extensive social provision. In these regulated and consensual social spheres, citizens have internalized the meanings and 'mattering maps' (Mann, 2005, 23) that prevail throughout the polity. Politics and other flows between civil society and the state are highly organized, offering the opportunity for effective and efficient attention to those whose voices can be heard. However, the downside of this kind of regime is its pre-emptive categorizing of interactions between the state and civil society, restricting fuller and informal public action.

These models of the state allow us to develop models of how education systems change. Educational policy interventions are situated within the broader regimes outlined earlier. Educational policy in laissez-faire regimes applies market principles to educational provision through school choice. School choice is informed through the publication of test results, which is the currency for users to make their choice and providers to allocate funds. Theoretically, the government's role is to protect and regulate the operation of these market forces. However, there are serious obstacles to the ideal operation of this approach, even if it is accepted that it is an appropriate way of providing public education. At its best, it is only a quasi-market because users have unequal access to schools, many being constrained by a lack of mobility, resources and the cultural codes they employ. Thus, the state has to intervene to compensate for rigidities in the liberal operation of the system. The driving force of these tests, and their use for mainly accountability considerations rather than scholastic improvement, has also corrupted the capacity of schools for developing teaching and learning programmes. Market models of education supposedly determine content through parental choice, but the fact that some parents are more vocal than others in expressing preferences means that the state has to step in, again undermining notions of consumer choice. In the United States, school boards decide on specific content under national guidelines; in Britain, the central government has developed a national curriculum. The laissez-faire regime has been associated historically with a 'back-to-basics agenda'. Teachers lose ground as a professional group in the market model to national regulation of school choice, privileging parents, examiners and evaluators. Parental demands and external accountability mechanisms take precedence over teachers' efforts to improve learning.

Again, consistent with top-down corporatism, teacher accountability is strong but is mainly an accountability directed at the corporation rather than the clients. It tends to be discretionary because of patrimonial loyalties, even where, as in Mexico, it occurs through high-stakes standardized testing. Here teachers' tenure deflects motivation or sanction by results. Depending on the balance of power between the corporation and the authorities, the teachers' corporation/official union may have to accept non-market incentives through periodic examinations or tests. Poor results lead to teachers taking refresher courses. In Mexico, the adoption of standardized tests fitted perfectly well within the framework of appearing to take teacher accountability seriously, even if there was no evidence for improved teaching and learning, the sanction of firing being obviated by tenure. This type of motivational mechanism is undermined when the process takes place within house, favourable or unfavourable relations leading to cronyism and corruption. In Mexico currently, the weakening of the union is bearing down on tenure and poorly formulated programmes of learning. Unfortunately, it is doing little to improve working conditions, since, like many government bureaucracies, its input to educational improvement processes, unlike that of the teaching workforce, is far less accountable and even less subject to public scrutiny. Moreover, adherence to the top-down approach ignores the fact that local events generate or construct conditions or structures that have consequences far removed from them. In the real world, they are active agents that may act in a variety of ways in response to reforms, changes, innovations and programmes. They may initiate reforms, sponsor or sustain them or actively subvert them. But this energy cannot be harnessed by those agents and agencies responsible for the process, which operates from above.

In protectionist policy regimes, educational policy development is also centralized because the nation state seeks to bind together diverse segments of the population by setting curriculum, administrative and in some cases, as in the corporatist regimes, pedagogical conditions for action. Nevertheless, the very cultural and social class distinctions that pervade the society require the diversification of provision and the authorization of private and independent provision, consistent with the neoliberalism prevalent in many previously protectionist economies. There is an active presence of the private and independent sectors in the provision of education, especially for religious and ethnic minorities as well as for the poor and marginalized. This effervescence points up the tension between the public and private sectors and between the centre and periphery. Depending on the degree of decentralization of the public educational administration to the regions, friction may exist both *between* these levels and *within* the public sector. And depending on the degree of centralization, in this regime, teachers are likely to be subject to similar state professionalization interventions as in the corporatist regime.

Prominent interventions are training, accountability and standardized promotion and benefits (though as in the corporatist regime, these may be cross-cut by patronage). A national curriculum is typical of this regime, though concessions may be made to local and minority interests in relation to content and operational style. In the protectionist regimes, the union may well have become a powerful special interest group, especially where civil society has become vocal and active, and where, due to its size, it has significant presence in the educational system. However, because it is not incorporated into the system as an official union, then, as a part of the bureaucracy, its relationship with that bureaucracy is different and does not depend on corporate agreements, the trade-offs so characteristic of official unions.

In developmentalist states, educational policy development is also centralized, in part because the nation state seeks to bind together diverse segments of the population. The main reason for centralization stems from the strong planning imperative of developmentalist states where education is articulated in relation to the broader economic goals of the nation. Nevertheless, the very cultural and social class distinctions that pervade the society require the diversification of provision, albeit under guidelines stipulated by the central authority. The protagonistic role of the state in promoting economic development through focused partnerships with the business world leaves its mark on educational policy.

Close attention is paid in the developmentalist states to policy implementation and improving performance standards, and these are built into the system through advanced preparation of teachers and other educational professions. Performance monitoring is helped by coordinating bodies like national institutes of education that work to maintain coherence within the educational system and with the broader planning of the economy as a whole. The pragmatic coordination of education under centralized management has invited strong criticisms of students and teachers being inserted into a system, allowing them little individuality in what looks like a highly regimented educational approach. More recent attempts to encourage innovation and flexibility in teaching and learning are undermined by centralized coordination, derived from a pragmatic workforce-planning approach to education.

In social democratic regimes, the state's chief purpose is to ensure that education is provided to all citizens and is of comparable if not equal quality, as the basis for a stable, well-provided, democracy. Unlike laissez-faire societies, the regime considers that the market is unreliable, inappropriate and even negatively attuned to the provision of education, considering it a public good in Adam Smith's terms ([1776] (1977)).

It is thus segregated from the provision of consumer and capital goods, where the market can be relied on. Two elements characterize educational policies in this regime. The first of these is the preparation of teachers through advanced, university-level, training, at an equivalent level to the preparation of other professionals. This encourages high performance levels, rewarded by high salaries, again in line with other professionals, and it enhances teachers' status, prestige and thus motivation in the society. And secondly, there is broad participation in the operation of the educational process both as an expression of the democratic and inclusive principles of the regime as a whole and also as a way of co-opting valuable partners into the educational process, thereby maintaining its quality and value in society. Evaluative mechanisms of teachers and students rely on classroom performance and formative assessment processes; standardized testing being treated with suspicion and seen as divisive, bringing in competitive market principles into a field in which their influence is considered destructive.

In corporative-clientelist regimes, the flow of policy is top-down from the state or international institutions, that is, those forces emanating from the higher levels of the system cause or determine actions at the lower end and constrain local actions. Nevertheless, the power of official and corporative unions, in this case the teachers' unions, obliges the state to negotiate over most key areas of education: teachers' service conditions, the curriculum, evaluation processes and teacher training. These policies are frequently preceded by pacts, agreements or alliances made at the top level at the onset of policy reforms. Additionally, at all levels of the educational bureaucracy, policy measures become tradable entities over which different groups wrestle to gain advantages or establish loyalties and exchange favours. The substantive aspects of educational policies thus give way to political considerations of a corporatist and clientelist nature. Policies are drained of educational content. This means that the official organization schedule is a very imperfect guide to real policy flows. This results in actual practice in the classroom bearing little resemblance to original top-level intentions. At the school level, educators, exhausted by the continuous flow of endlessly changing and ineffective policies, tend to take the easiest option, which is to delay and prevaricate.

Educational development

In Margaret Archer's (2013) domain theory of educational development, the emergence of state educational systems is seen as the final phase of a morphogenetic cycle. This meta-theoretical framework indicates that structural changes in society, or parts of it, can be studied as sequences of morphogenetic cycles, where the last phase in one cycle constitutes the first phase in the next cycle. The model incorporates historical time as a variable, and the different phases in a cycle extend over different but overlapping time tracts. Structure exists prior to interaction and structural change is the (often unintended) result of interaction. Guided by this model, the study of structural change entails the identification of morphogenetic cycles and their three phases: structural conditioning, social interaction and morphogenesis.

In Archer's terms, *structural conditioning* necessarily pre-dates actions that either reproduce (they are *morphostatic*) or elaborate on structures (they are *morphogenetic*) and focus on which humans may or may not be reflexive in the course of this *sociocultural interaction*. Reflexivity is a key aspect of morphogenesis; the conditions for a morphogenetic society are furthered by individuals becoming more self-directed and therefore reflexive. Archer (2007, 46) argues that contrary to previous historical periods, we are now in a situation in which 'structure and culture have come into synergy with one another with far-reaching morphogenetic consequences'. Her argument is that in previous eras cultures were contained within the bounds of structure, resulting in morphostasis or 'cultural/social maintenance'. Over the last generation, however, culture and structure have converged so as to promote morphogenesis.

Change

We also need to make sense of the notion of change or alteration. Objects and relations between objects, educational systems and people change their form over time. An example of this change process at the epistemological level is the invention (insofar as the set of concepts and relations between them is new) of the notion of probability (see also Hacking, 1999) in the nineteenth century, and this changed the way social objects could be conceived and ultimately arranged. Change can occur in four ways: contingent ontological, planned ontological, epistemically driven ontological and in the transitive realm of knowledge, epistemological (see also Scott, 2011). With regards to the example above, the invention of probability, two phases of change can be identified. The first is where knowledge is created and thus operates at the epistemological level, the new arrangement of knowledge. The second is where this knowledge has real effects at the ontological level, so that new arrangements, new formations, new assemblages come into being. The dilemma is that the social world, in contrast to the physical world, is always in a state of transition and flux, so that it is hard to argue that there are invariant laws by which the world works, at all times and in all places, except in a basic logical and rational sense.

Society is characterized by notions of continuous emergence, flux and change. Objects in the world cannot be characterized by their essential qualities, but only through their interactions with other objects. Complexity resides in all these various interactions which produce new objects (characterized as different forms of structure), and results in a bewildering array of arrangements of material and human objects. Because they are difficult to characterize they rarely allow definitive accounts of what is going on to be produced. It is the complexity of these object interactions and their subsequent and temporary coalescences that makes it difficult to provide complete descriptions of them. The epistemic level is unsynchronized with the ontic level because researchers and investigators have not developed sufficiently their instruments and conceptual schema for capturing something that is both ever-changing and has too many elements to it, that is, it is too complex. However, this does not categorically rule out the possibility of providing more complete descriptions of events, structures, mechanisms and their relations in the world. This suggests a notion of human fallibility, which means that human actions are corrigible. The twin elements of complexity and temporal emergence cannot preclude correct descriptions being made of activities in the world, only that these elements can create considerable difficulties. This is further compounded by how emergence operates in the world.

Many theorists go further than this (for example, Osberg and Biesta, 2007), and hold to a version of emergence in which there is a radical incommensurability between different formations over time (whether material, embodied or discursive). Furthermore, it is impossible to predict what interconnections, new formations and iterations of the object system will be realized, because the principles of the new mechanism are not given in the current arrangements. In other words, the relations between objects and the objects themselves, which make up activity systems, are not patterned in any meaningful sense; there is a radical incommensurability between these different iterations.

All discussions of a person or an education system over time require some understanding of change; that is, the notion of change is built into the conception of the human being or system. There is also the problem of persistence. If there was no cohering element between moments, so that every moment entails a change of person or system, we would not have a sense of personhood or system identity, which therefore has to include a notion of persistence over time, and, in addition, has a notion of emergence. And this is emergence understood in its two modes: as a temporal phenomenon and ontologically, as a response to the stratified nature of reality.

Insight into problems faced by an education system and awareness of potential solutions do not necessarily lead to the ability to act in an effective manner in order to guide stakeholders in instituting a change. The rapid and successful implementation of reforms in a school system is directly dependent on the quality of the knowledge, skills and thinking that a system and those that introduce its planned reforms bring to the reform process. Moreover, innovations and reforms call for new, and often substantially improved, knowledge, skills and thinking in several domains. This includes knowledge about obstacles to change at both the instrumental and affective levels and about the change process itself.

Education policies and practices in Mexico

In every social entity, the key to understanding educational institutions and practices is the nature of the new or professional middle class. This has been defined in European societies as both the author and beneficiary of education. In the case of Mexico, we have found that its search for cultural capital goes far beyond that of their European counterparts because in the past other avenues were not as readily available. We also found that this middle class is different because it is also created by the state and therefore doubly beholden to it. We suggested this could explain the apparent disparity between an often-revolutionary rhetoric and a distinctly conservative-oriented set of practices.

In the literature, the descriptive term 'middle class' is generally used in two different yet sometimes overlapping ways. The first refers to those who have accumulated physical capital largely through their activities as small entrepreneurs, and related professionals and managers. They are not necessarily independent of large state-run or state-sponsored bodies in a large number of countries where the state formally and informally is sometimes indistinguishable from what are the productive sectors. They do not often achieve the relative political independence from the state that is a characteristic of Anglo-Saxon and European countries. The second refers to those who have accumulated cultural capital, as is the case of Mexico, and have been created by and/or are dependent on the state. They are charged with managing state institutions and include associated professionals usually certified by state bodies. The dual need of establishing and preserving institutions that allow the accumulation of cultural capital highlights the importance of educational institutions for this group.

In part, a sotto voce theme in the development of Latin American societies has been the middle classes striving for self-certification as well as developing those institutions that would underwrite that process. So long as the middle class was a junior partner its voice could not be heard, nor could it constitute the types of alliances that the middle classes were able to achieve in Europe, because their potential allies were seen as enemies of the state and were suppressed by middle-class institutions. Radical middle-class organizations that strongly influenced if not dominated public discourse like the Fabian Society in Britain had and have no real counterpart outside the academic world in countries like Mexico. Only when the stability guaranteeing social peace seemed to become permanent after 1946 and the state-provided training institutions became more professional was the middle class able to even begin to imagine establishing its own hegemony and dream more realistically about becoming independent of the state. The process was accelerated by competition for positions and the effects of world trade agreements, and therefore the Mexican middle class gravitated towards the right of the political spectrum, strongly conditioned by its wish to transfer cultural capital into physical capital.

In the light of what for many was the hoped-for eclipse of the corporativist state, as a result of the election in 2000, the door was open to such changes. At first glance the Mexican middle class appeared to be in a better position to mould institutions and practices according to its image. The victory of the right-of-centre National Action Party was therefore an important step in that process and its educational programme a recognition of that important change. Ironically, at least for a time, it also freed the middle classes from a contradictory *Weltanschauung* and opened the door on empirical research, which, if we take the work of Carlos Muñoz Izquierdo (2009) as an example, revealed the catastrophic failure of the educational system to deliver. However, the contradiction between a middle class formed by cultural capital and one formed by physical capital remained, the new regime accommodated to the corporative institutional arrangements. The struggle proved to be a much more complex one than found in Europe and was reflected in the very policies and administrative procedures of the new government.

Hence, from 2000 to 2012, with the election of Vicente Fox, the standard bearer of the Partido de Acción Nacional (PAN), as president, followed by Felipe Calderón Hinojosa in 2006, for the first time since 1917 the groups that coalesced into the Partido de la Revolución Mexicana (the aptly named Institutional Revolutionary Party) were no longer in power. But the transition from a corporativist state to what the new leaders described as a liberal democracy never took place. Institutional continuity was maintained and the agencies continued to operate much as before. We have suggested that the agencies were never designed for implementation but for the maintenance by default of the status quo and that these agencies themselves have absorbed the professional middle classes to such an extent that the new middle classes perceive any such changes as against their interests.

As a result of our analysis of education in Mexico we suggest that future research and the construction of educational reform programmes need to take into account the following: an educational process cannot be analysed as institutions and practices removed from the socio-economic context in which they are situated; educational processes are political sites involved in the construction and control of discourse, meaning and subjectivities, and the common-sense values and beliefs that guide and structure any educational practice are not a priori universals, but social constructions based on specific normative and political assumptions. We should never take these for granted and should regard them, as Bourdieu (2005) argues, as 'cultural arbitraries'.

The structural theorists of modern anthropology have analysed what they call social apprenticeship in this way. More recently, social research has moved in that direction. We hope that in this work we have provided sufficient empirically based evidence for the development of a fruitful dialogue between these two hitherto different approaches that will enhance our understanding of education institutions and practices and help us to overcome the in-built and seemingly insuperable obstacles to the implementation of equitable, viable and sustainable educational reforms.

Since Gilberto Guevara (1992) published his essays on educational failure in the Mexican system, many Mexican and overseas commentators are aghast at what appears to be a dysfunctional system that has impeded the country from moving up the sacred performance league table of education achievement set by the OECD. However, they miss the point that in terms of its original purpose, it was not one of selection but of emphasizing social control and in that sense, it has been mostly successful. Indeed, in socio-anthropological terms no institution is ever dysfunctional. By layering institution upon institution as occurs every sexenio, to the extent that in one of the larger states there were 17 organizations set up at different times to research curriculum innovation, has the advantage of providing real and phantom jobs to satisfy the thirst for patronage, but obviously makes such research impossible. At a certain point reality has to creep in and lead to the conclusion that the greatest impediment to a meaningful education are the institutions themselves that deal with this important area of social life. Defining the obstacle is perhaps the first step in finding a way forward.

This study, in part, has had the middle class as its protagonist. By focusing on its constitution, its vicissitudes and alliances one can begin to form a clearer picture of the evolution of Mexican society that goes beyond the historical myths that were created to build and maintain a sense of nationhood. Aside from some of the biographical studies of Enrique Krauze (1997, 2008) and hints in the writing of other commentators, we have no studies that are anything more than anecdotal. A final irony is that in these unequal and heterogeneous societies, the new or professional middle class as we have defined it at the outset of this work is essential if meaningful reforms are to be put into practice. Because of changes in the division of labour that require coordination, administration and aspects of social control, the non-entrepreneurial middle class has become increasingly important for the functioning of systems of mechanical solidarity. These changes coincided not only with their wish for professionalism but also for them a fortuitous change in the demands of the labour market that required more professionals. This is because it plays a crucial role in the authorship of educational systems and practices and also the champion and protector of much that is necessary in education. When, as is the case in most Latin American countries, the participation of the middle class in state education falls below a certain level, state education loses its cutting edge. The Fabian reformers and their allies in the educational world could only devise and enact those reforms which opened up schooling because of a solid middle class operating within certain historical determinants and because of its alliance with working-class organizations.

Until now in Mexico, not only has such an alliance been impossible but also, in addition, the new middle class, for historical and social reasons, sees the working class and, more importantly, the much larger sector constituting the marginal populations, as potential and dangerous competitors. In Mexico, the agents for such reforms are a tiny sector in which most of the professional middle class largely does not participate. Because of these assumptions, authority was not seen as delegated but treated as a synonym for power. The few historical studies of the evolution of national education systems are not entirely useful because they tend to operate within a functionalist model that assumes that once an institution is created, it has the scope and hence the freedom to make decisions independently. This means that the mainstream theoretical models that have been constructed do not help us to understand the origin of and changes in the relations between society and its systems of social apprenticeship. For that reason, they do not help us to recognize why most education reforms are not delivered in ways that are intended by the progenitors of these reforms. From the outset, the observations that were made of the growing influence of the state with its ability to penetrate into all walks of life, positively and negatively, established the basis for the idea of state neutrality and state intervention, which meant that the state could be seen as operating at a level above society and social conflict. These ideas solidified to constitute the basic assumptions of both social scientists and policymakers.

This conflating of bureaucratic ideals with actual practice is common in all branches of public policy writing. But it is also a view that enters into and fixes itself in the popular imagination. We tend to talk of the government or the state interchangeably (as if it was a unified entity or a person), deciding everything from the distribution of computers to schools to developing a new and supposedly more relevant curriculum. We assume that it will happen as it is planned. There may be obstacles, but we need to find ways to overcome them by fine-tuning and clarifying the rules for implementation, or so the thinking goes. It is common to see educational policy interventions or the external promotion of educational reforms as being without ulterior motives and above political and personal interests. But those who have been involved in policy development know that sooner or later they will find they are caught up in a complex web of social, economic and political cross-currents.

Hence, we need to analyse Mexican education as part of a whole social formation. This is what Pierre Bourdieu (2005) and with Passeron (1977), and Basil Bernstein (1998) have done, and we have drawn upon their work to advance parts of our argument. But this cannot be done in the abstract, which is why we have placed so much importance on field data and a conception of formal educational arrangements interacting with the informal, rather than arguing from formal educational policy downwards, thereby relegating and minimizing these other social entities.

References

Aguayo, S. (2008) *The Mexican Almanac*, Mexico City: Quezado.

Aguayo, S. (2010) *Vuelta en U*, Mexico, DF: Guía para Entender y Reactivar la Democracia Estancada, Taurus, Santillana Ediciones Generales.

Alba, Martçinez O. (2011) 'En la escuela . . . más allá del aula . . . haciendo lo que tenemos que hacer', Presentation at Second Congress of the Centro Educativo Narciso Bassols, Enseñar y Aprender Hoy, 17–18 June 2011, Queretaro, Mexico.

Aldáz, I. (1998) *Matemáticas y Etnomatemáticas*, Oaxaca de Juárez, Oaxaca: Unidad de Proyectos Estratégicos.

Alvarez, I. (2002) *Planificien y Desarrollo de Proyectos Sociales y Educativos*, Editorial: Limusa.

Antillón, J. I. (1964) *Los Relámpagos de Agosto*, México: Joaquín Mortiz.

Archer, M. (2007) *Making our Way through the World*, Cambridge: Cambridge University Press.

Archer, M. (2013) *Social Origins of Educational Systems* (2nd edition), London: Routledge.

Bakhurst, D. (2009) 'Reflections on activity theory', *Education Review*, 61, 2: 197–210.

Ball, S. (1994) *Education Reform: A Critical and Post-Structural Approach*, Buckingham: Open University Press.

Barba, B. (2010) 'Entre maestros: reforma de la formación docente en Aguascalientes: un análisis de su implementación', *Revista Mexicana de Investigación Educativa*, 15, 44: 251–75.

Barnard, W. (2004) 'Parent involvement in elementary school and educational attainment', *Children and Youth Services Review*, 26: 39–62.

Basañez, M. (1990) *El Pulso de los Sexenios, Veinte Años de Crisis en México*, México, DF: Siglo XXI.

Basave, A. (2010) *Mexicanidad y Esquizofrenia: Los Dos Rostros del Mexicano*, Mexico, DF: Editorial Océano de México.

Benda, J. (1927) *La Trahison des Clercs*, Paris: Grasset.

Berger, E. and Riojas-Cortez, M. (2015) *Parents as Partners in Education: Families and Schools Working Together*, London: Pearson.

Bernstein, B. (1998) *Pedagogy, Symbolic Control and Identity: Theory, Research and Critique*, London and New York: Routledge.

Bhaskar, R. (2010) *Reclaiming Reality* (2nd edition), London and New York: Routledge.

Bobbitt, J. F. (1913) 'Some general principles of management applied to the problems of city-school systems', in *The Supervision of City Schools; Twelfth Yearbook of the National Society for the Study of Education*, Bloomington III: Public School Publishing Company.

Bobbitt, J. F. (1918) *The Curriculum*, Boston: Houghton Mifflin.

Bobbitt, J. F. (1924) *How to Make a Curriculum*, Boston: Houghton Mifflin.

Bourdieu, P. (2005) 'The political field, the social field, and the journalistic field', in R. Benson and E. Neveu (eds.), *Bourdieu and the Journalistic Field* (pp.29–46), Cambridge: Polity Press.

Bourdieu, P. and Passeron, J-C. (1977) *Reproduction in Education, Society and Culture*, London: Sage Publications.

Bracho, T. and Zamudio, A. (1997) 'El gasto privado en educacion: Mexico', *Revista Mexicana de Investigacion Educativa*, 2, 4: 323–47.

Brandom, R. (2000) *Articulating Reasons: An Introduction to Inferentialism*, Cambridge, MA: Harvard University Press.

Bredo, E. (1999) 'Reconstructing educational psychology', in P. Murphy (ed.), *Learners, Learning and Assessment*, London: Sage.

Bruner, J. (1996) *The Culture of Education*, Cambridge, MA: Harvard University Press.

Burawoy, M. (2009) *The Extended Case Method: Four Countries, Four Decades, Four Great Transformations, and One Theoretical Tradition*, Oakland, CA: University of California Press.

Castells, M. (1996) *The Rise of the Network Society, The Information Age: Economy, Society and Culture, Vol. I*. Cambridge, MA; Oxford, UK: Blackwell.

Cero en Conducta (1985) *La Revolucion Educativa*, 1.1, September–October, Educación y Cambio.

Charters, W. (1909) *Methods of Teaching: Developed from a Functional Standpoint*, Chicago: Row, Peterson and Company.

Charters, W. (1923) *Curriculum Construction*, New York: Macmillan.

Coordinación Nacional del Servicio Profesional Docente (CNSPD) (2015) *Programa de Promoción en la Función por Incentivos en Educación Básica*, Mexico City: Secretaria de Educación Publica.

Cowen, M. and Shenton, R. (2003) *Doctrines of Development*, London: Routledge.

Dearing, E., Kreider, H., Simpkins, S. and Weiss, H. B. (2006) 'Family involvement in school and low-income children's literacy: Longitudinal associations between and within families', *Journal of Educational Psychology*, 98: 653–64.

Diaz Barriga, A. (ed.) (2003) *Curricular Research in Mexico: The Decade of the Nineties*, Educative Research in Mexico Collection, volume 5, Mexico City: Mexican Council of Educative Research.

Diaz Barriga, A., Barron, C., Carlos, J. and Diaz Barriga, F. (1995) 'Research in the curricular field 1982–1992', in A. Diaz Barriga (ed.), *Curricular, Institutional and Organisational Processes*, Mexico City: Mexican Council of Educational Research.

Diaz Barriga, F. (2007) 'Main trends of curriculum research in Mexico', in W. Pinar (ed.), *International Handbook of Curriculum Research*, Mahwah, NJ.: Lawrence Erlbaum.

Domina, T. (2005) 'Levelling the home advantage: Assessing the effectiveness of parental involvement in elementary school', *Sociology of Education*, 78: 233–49.

Dore, R. (1976) *The Diploma Disease: Education, Qualification, and Development*, Berkeley: University of California Press.

Douglas, M. (2002) *Purity and Danger*, London: Routledge and Kegan Paul.

Durkheim, E. [1895] (1982) *The Rules of Sociological Method*, with an introduction by Steven Lucas, translated by W. D. Halls, New York: The Free Press.

Edge, K., Tao, S., Riley, K. and Khamsi, K. (2008) 'Teacher quality and parental participation: An exploratory review of research and resources related to influencing student outcomes', *The London Centre for Leadership in Learning*, Institute of Education, University of London.

Engeström, Y. (2001) 'Expansive learning at work: Toward an activity theoretical reconceptualization', *Journal of Education and Work*, 14, 1: 133–56.

Epstein, J. (2010) 'School/family/community partnerships: Caring for the children we share', *Phi Delta Kappan*, 92, 3: 81–96.

Ezpeleta, J. (1990) 'El Consejo Técnico: eficacia pedagógica y estructura de poder en la escuela primaria Mexicana', *Revista Latinoamericano de Estudios Educativos*, XX, 4: 13–33.

Ezpeleta, J. (2004) 'Innovaciones educativas: Reflexiones sobre los contextos en su implementación', *RMEI*, 9, 21: 403–24.

Financial Times (2 June 2015) 'Mexico takes gamble on suspending key pillar of education reform', available at http://www.ft.com/cms/s/0/2b1780d8-0898-11e5-b38c-00144feabdc0.html#axzz3iKGa3bwZ, accessed 7 August 2015.

Financial Times (22 July 2015) 'Teachers' union raises stakes in battle with Mexico's Peña Nieto', available at http://www.ft.com/cms/s/0/640d606e-3044-11e5-8873-775ba7c2ea3d.html#axzz3iKGa3bwZ, accessed 7 August 2015.

Flores Andrade, A. (2014) 'Fundamental aspects of general law of professional teaching service 2013 in Mexico', *Iberofórum*, 17: 174–202.

Fortoul, O. (2014) 'La reforma integral de la educación básica y la formación de maestros', *Perfiles Educativos*, 36, 143: 46–55.

Foster, G. (1965) 'Peasant society and the image of limited good', *American Anthropologist*, 67, 2: 293–315.

Freinet, C. (1993) *Education Through Work: A Model for Child-Centered Learning*, translated by John Sivell, Lewiston: Edwin Mellen Press.

Freire, P. (1970) *Pedagogy of the Oppressed*, New York: Herder and Herder.

Fullan, M. and Hargreaves, A. (1996) *What's Worth Fighting for in Your School*, New York: Teachers College, Columbia University.

Furlan, A. (2011) 'Curriculum studies in Mexico: Key scholars', in W. Pinar (ed.), *Curriculum Studies in Mexico: Intellectual Histories, Present Circumstances*, London: Palgrave Macmillan.

Gago, A. (1982) *Development of Descriptive Letters*, Mexico City: Trillas.

Glazman, R. and de Ibarrola, M. (1976) *Design of Study Plans*, Mexico City: CISE/UNAM.
Gonzalez-DeHass, A., Willems, P. and Holbein, M. (2005) 'Examining the relationship between parental involvement and student motivation', *Educational Psychology Review*, 17, 2: 99–111.
Government of Mexico (2004) *Comprehensive Reform of Basic Education (Reforma Integral de la Educación Básica (RIEB))*, Mexico City: Government of Mexico.
Government of Mexico (2013) *Ley General del Servicio Profesional Docente (LGSPD)*, Mexico City: Secretaria de Servicios Parlamentarios.
Gramsci, A. (1971) *Selections from the Prison Notebooks*, New York: International Publishers.
Green, A. and Janmaat, J. (2014) *Regimes of Social Cohesion: Societies and the Crisis of Globalization*, London: Palgrave Macmillan.
Grindle, M. (1977) *Bureaucrats, Politicians, and Peasants in Mexico: A Case Study in Public Policy*, Los Angeles: University of California Press.
Guevara Niebla, G. (ed.) (1981) *La Crisis de la Educación Superior en México*, Mexico, DF: Editorial Nueva Imagen.
Guevara Niebla, G. (1992) *La CatráStrofe Silencosa*, Mexico, DF: FCE.
Hacking, I. (1999) *The Social Construction of What?* Cambridge, MA: Harvard University Press.
Halsey, A. H., Heath, A. and Ridge, J. (1980) *Origins and Destinations*, Oxford: Clarendon.
Hassrick, E. and Schneider, B. (2009) 'Parent surveillance in schools: A question of social class', *American Journal of Education*, 115, 2: 195–225.
Held, D., Goldblatt, D., McGrew, A. and Perraton, J. (1999) *Global Transformations: Politics, Economics and Culture*, Stanford, CA: Stanford University Press.
Hoover-Dempsey, K., Walker, J., Sandler, H., Whetsel, D., Green, C., Wilkins, A. and Closson, K. (2005) 'Why do parents become involved? Research findings and implications', *The Elementary School Journal*, 106, 2: 105–30.
Huerta, J. (1981) *Logical Organisation of Learning Experiences*, Mexico City: Trillas.
Illich, I. (1971) *Deschooling Society*, New York: Harper and Row.
Instituto Nacional de Estadística y Geografía (INEGI) (2013) *Classes Medias en México*, Mexico City: Instituto Nacional de Estadística y Geografía (INEGI), retrieved 19 July 2013.
Instituto Nacional para la Evaluación de la Educación (2016) *Los Docentes en México, Informe 2016*, Mexico: INEE.
Jeynes, W. (2010) 'The salience of the subtle aspects of parental involvement and encouraging that involvement: Implications for school-based programs', *The Teachers College Record*, 112, 3: 45–67.
Jeynes, W. (2011) *Parental Involvement and Academic Success*, New York: Routledge.
Jones, R. (2001) 'How parents can support learning: Not all parent involvement programs are equal, but research shows what works', *American School Board Journal*, 188, 9: 18–22.
Krauze, E. (1976) *Caudillos Culturales en la Revolución Mexican*, México: Siglo XXI.
Krauze, E. (1997) *Mexico: Biography of Power. A History of Modern Mexico, 1810–1996*, New York: HarperCollins.
Krauze, E. (2008) *El Poder y el Delirio*, Mexico City: Tusquets Editores.
Kumar, A. (2011) 'Curriculum studies in Mexico: An overview', in W. Pinar (ed.), *Curriculum Studies in Mexico: Intellectual Histories, Present Circumstances*, London: Palgrave Macmillan.
Lankshear, C., Peters, M. and Knobel, M. (1996) 'Critical pedagogy and cyberspace', in H. Giroux, with C. Lankshear, P. McLaren and M. Peters (eds.), *Counternarratives: Cultural Studies and Critical Pedagogies in Postmodern Spaces*, New York and London: Routledge.
Lasch, C. (1979) *The Culture of Narcissism*, London: W. W. Norton and Company.
Latour, B. (1987) *Science in Action: How to Follow Scientists and Engineers Through Society*, Milton Keynes: Open University Press.
Lave, J. and Wenger, E. (1991) *Situated Learning: Legitimate Peripheral Participation*, Cambridge: Cambridge University Press.
Leonardo, de, P. (1983) *La Educación Superior Privada en México: Bosquejo Histórico*, Serie Estado y Educación en Mexico, Mexico City: Editorial Línea.
Lingard, B. (2000) 'It is and it isn't: Vernacular globalisation', in N. Burbles and C. Torres (eds.), *Globalisation and Education: Critical Perspectives* (pp. 275–96), London: Routledge.
Lomnitz, C. (2000) *Deep Mexico, Silent Mexico, An Anthropology of Nationalism*, Oakland, CA: University of California Press.
Lugaz, C. and De Grauwe, A. (eds.) (2010) *Schooling and Decentralisation: Patterns and Policy Implications in Francophone West Africa*, Paris: International Institute for Educational Planning (IIEP), UNESCO.

Maandag, D., Deinum, J., Hofman, W. and Buitink, J. (2007) 'Teacher education in schools: An international comparison', *European Journal of Teacher Education*, 3, 2: 151–73.

Mann, M. (2005) *The Dark Side of Democracy: Explaining Ethnic Cleansing*, Cambridge: Cambridge University Press.

Mars, G. (1982) *Cheats at Work: An Anthropology of Workplace Crime*, London: Allen and Unwin.

Martin, C. (2004) *La Educación Primaria en Tiempos de Eusteridad*, Aula XXI, Mexico, DF: Santillana.

Martin, C. (2007) 'The reform for EFA in Mexico', in D. P. Baker and A. W. Wiseman (eds.), *Education for All: Global Promises, National Changes*, volume 8, chapter 7, Oxford, UK: Elsevier Science Ltd.

Martin, C. and Guzman, E. (2016) 'Parental participation in schooling: A divorce of convenience', *Sinectica*, 46, available at https://sinectica.iteso.mx/index.php/SINECTICA/article/view/628, accessed 15 March 2016.

Martínez Bordon, A., Bracho González, T. and Osiris Martínez Valle, C. (2007) *Los Consejos de Participación Social en la Educación y el Programa Escuelas de Calidad: ¿Mecanismos Sociales para la Rendición de Cuentas?* CIESAS y Universidad Autónoma de Veracruz.

Martínez, O. (2009) *Un Futuro para la Escuela Pública*, Mexico, DF: Ediciones de Educación y Cultura.

McLaren, P. (1989) *Life in Schools*, New York: Longman.

Mercado, R. (2010) *Investigadora Convestav Doctoraen Ciencias en la Especialidad de Investigadora Educativas*, DIE-Cinvestav.

Merleau-Ponty, M. [1945] (1962) *Phenomenology of Perception*, translated by Colin Smith, New York: Humanities Press and London: Routledge.

Messick, S. (1989) 'Validity', in R. Linn (ed.), *Educational Measurement* (3rd edition), Washington, DC: American Council on Education.

Meyer, J. (1973) *La Révolution Mexicaine 1910–1940*, Paris: Calmann Lévy.

Muñoz Izquierdo, C. (2009) *Como Puede la Educacieon Contribuir a la Movilidad Social?: Resultados de Cuarto Décadas de Investigación Sobre la Calidad y los Efectos Socioeconómicos de la Educación (1968–2008)*, Mexico City, DA: Universidad Iberoamericana Biblioteca Francisco Xavier Clavigero.

Noah, H. and Eckstein, M. (1969) *Toward a Science of Comparative Education*, New York: Macmillan.

Organisation for Economic Co-operation and Development (OECD) (2012) *Mexico: Education at a Glance*, Paris: OECD.

Organisation for Economic Co-operation and Development (OECD) (2013) *Mexico*, Paris: OECD.

Ornelas, C. (2008) *Política, Poder y Pupitres: Crítica al Nuevo Federalismo Educativo*, Mexico City: Siglo Veintiuno Editores.

Ornelas, C. (2012) *Educación, Colonización y Rebeldía: La Herencia del Pacto Calderón-Gordillo*, Mexico: Siglo XXI.

Ornelas, C. (2014) *Educación y Participación Social*, available at http://www.excelsior.com.mx/opinion/carlos-ornelas/2014/03/12/948225, accessed 12 March 2014.

Ortiz González, M. (1998) *¿Dónde Está el Porvenir? Las Expectativas de los Jóvenes Hacia el Trabajo Local, la Educación y la Migración en Tizapán el Alto Jalisco*, Tesis de Maestría, Departamento de Estudios de Educación, Universidad de Guadalajara.

Osberg, D. and Biesta, G. (2007) 'Beyond presence: epistemological and pedagogical implications of strong emergence', *Interchange*, 38, 1: 31–51.

Paz, O. (1994) *The Labyrinth of Solitude: The Other Mexico, Return to the Labyrinth of Solitude, Mexico and the United States, the Philanthropic Ogre*, New York: Grove Press.

Popham, W. H. (1972) *An Evaluation Guidebook: A Set of Practical Guidelines for the Educational Evaluator*, Los Angeles: The Instructional Objectives Exchange.

Posner, C., Martin, C. and Guzman, E. (2017) *Education in Latin American Countries*, London: Bloomsbury.

Reich, R. (2015) *Saving Capitalism: For the Many, Not the Few*, New York: Knopf Publishing Group.

Remedi, E. (1999) 'Ralph Tyler: A notable encounter', in A. Furlan and M. Pasillas (eds.), *Ralph Tyler: Lectures Committed to Forty Years from "Basic Principles of Curriculum"*, Mexico City: The Autonomous University of Sinaloa.

Rodríguez-Gómez, R. (2015) 'El proyecto educativo SEP-SNTE y la prueba ENLACE', *Revista Mexicana de Investigación Educativa*, 20, 64: 309–24, available at http://www.ses.unam.mx/integrantes/uploadfile/rrodriguez/Rodriguez2015_ElProyectoEducativo.pdf, accessed 1 September 2015.

Rodrik, D. (2008) *One Economics, Many Recipes: Globalization, Institutions, and Economic Growth*, Princetown: Princetown University Press.

Santillán Nieto, M. (2012) *La Formación Docente en México*, Dirección General de Educación Superior para Profesionales de la Educación, available at https://www.oecd.org/edu/school/43765204.pdf, accessed 23 June 2017.

Santizo Rodall, C. (2010) *Guía para Promover la Participación Social en los Procesos de Tomas de Decisiones de las Escuelas*, mimeo, México, DF: Universidad Autónoma Metropolitana, Cuajimalpa.

Santizo Rodall, C. (2011) 'Gobernanza y participación social en la escuela publica', *RMIE*, 16, 50: 751–73.

Schon, D. (2005) *The Reflective Practitioner: How Professionals Think in Action*, San Francisco: Jossey-Bass.

Schwille, J. and Dembélé, M. (2007) *Global Perspective on Teacher Learning; Improving Policy and Practice*, Paris: IIEP/UNESCO.

Scott, D. (2011) *Education, Epistemology and Critical Realism*, London and New York: Routledge.

Scott, D., Posner, C., Martin, C., Guzman Flores, E., Alvarez-M, O., Zotzmann, K., Encinas, M., Demetriou, A., Alvarez, F., Andrews, R., Houssart, J. and Dale-Tunnicliffe, S. (2012) *Final Report: Research and Developments Project: Curriculum Standards*, Mexico: Ministry of Education.

Scott, J. (1985) *Everyday Forms of Peasant Resistance*, New Haven, CT: Yale University Press.

Scott, J. (2010) *The Art of Not Being Governed: An Anarchist History of Upland Southeast Asia*, Yale Agrarian Studies Series, New Haven, CT: Yale University Press.

Secretaría de Educación Pública (2009) *Report*, available at http://www.consejosescolares.sep.gob.mx/work/models/conapase/Resource/84/1/images/ACUERDO%20716.pdf, accessed 23 June 2017.

Secretaría de Educación Pública (2014) *Acuerdo Número 716 por el que se Establecen los Lineamientos para la Constitución, Organización y Funcionamiento de los Consejos de Participación Social en la Educación*, available at http://www.consejosescolares.sep.gob.mx/work/models/conapase/Resource/84/1/images/ACUERDO%20716.pdf, accessed 23 June 2017.

Senate of the Republic (2013) 'Dictamen de las Comisiones Unidas de Educación y de Estudios Legislativos, con Proyecto de Decreto por el que se expide la Ley General del Servicio Profesional Docente', Mexico City: Government of Mexico.

Smith, A. [1776] (1977) *An Enquiry into the Nature and Causes of the Wealth of Nations*, Chicago: University of Chicago Press.

Street, S. (2001) 'When politics becomes pedagogy: Oppositional discourse as policy in Mexican teachers' struggles for union democracy', in M. Sutton and B. Levinson (eds.), *Policy as Practice: Towards a Comparative Sociocultural Analysis of Educational Policy* (pp. 145–66), Westport, CT: Ablex.

Sutton, M. and Levinson, B. (eds.) (2001) *Policy as Practice: Towards a Comparative Sociocultural Analysis of Educational Policy*, Westport, CT: Ablex.

Tertulia IV, DF. (2012) *Annual Meeting of La Tertulia in Mexico*, Mexico City: La Tertulia.

The Commission for New Teaching Methods (1976) *Programmed Teaching*, Mexico City: CNME/UNAM.

Touraine, A. (1971) *The Post-Industrial Society; Tomorrow's Social History: Classes, Conflicts and Culture in the Programmed Society*, New York: Random House.

Tyler, R. (1950) *Basic Principles of Curriculum and Instruction*, Chicago, IL: University of Chicago Press.

Tyler, R. (1968) *The Challenge of National Assessment*, Columbus, OH: Charles E. Merrill Publishing Company.

United Nations Educational, Scientific and Cultural Organization (UNESCO) (2013) *Education Policy Outlook Mexico*, Paris: OECD.

Verduzco, I. and Tapia, M. (2012) 'Organizaciones de la sociedad civil: presentes en las escuelas, ausentes de las políticas educativas', Mexico City: Alternativas y Capacidades, A.C.

Vygotsky, L. (1978) *Mind in Society: The Development of Higher Psychological Processes*, in M. Cole, V. John-Steirner and S. Scribner (eds.), Cambridge, MA: Harvard University Press.

Whitty, G., Power, S. and Halpin, D. (1998) *Devolution and Choice in Education: The School, the State and the Market*, Buckingham: Open University Press.
Winch, C. (2014) 'Education and broad concepts of agency', *Educational Philosophy and Theory*, 48, 6: 569–83.
World Economic Forum (2016–17), *Report*, Geneva: World Economic Forum.
Zermeno, H. and Torres Medina, J. (2005) *Mexico: de la Reforma y el Imperio*, Naucalpan de Juarez: Universidad Nacional Autonoma de Mexico, Facultad de Estudios Superiores Acatlan.
Zurita, R., José, U., Velasco, L., Soca de Iñigo, J. and Viviana Pin To, L. (2003) *La Participación Social en las Escuelas Primarias del Distrito Federal*, Mexico City: Government of Mexico.

Index

www.ingramcontent.com/pod-product-compliance
Lightning Source LLC
LaVergne TN
LVHW010731020926
846742LV00029B/43